LEARNING TO
Dance
IN THE RAIN II

LEARNING TO
Dance
IN THE RAIN II

Surviving Grief, Internet Dating and Romance Scams!

SHELBY WAGNER

Copyright © 2020 by Shelby Wagner.

Library of Congress Control Number: 2020923894
ISBN: Hardcover   978-1-6641-4590-0
               Softcover   978-1-6641-4589-4
               eBook   978-1-6641-4588-7

All rights reserved. No part of this book may be reproduced or transmitted in any form or by any means, electronic or mechanical, including photocopying, recording, or by any information storage and retrieval system, without permission in writing from the copyright owner.

Any people depicted in stock imagery provided by Getty Images are models, and such images are being used for illustrative purposes only.
Certain stock imagery © Getty Images.

Print information available on the last page.

Rev. date: 01/27/2021

To order additional copies of this book, contact:
Xlibris
844-714-8691
www.Xlibris.com
Orders@Xlibris.com
818634

REVIEWS

"I found this book to be very insightful and filled with important information regarding what to look for when participating in the dating scene, especially as a senior woman. It provides valuable tools and strategies when communicating with people on social media. Since I had been defrauded of a lot of money in a dating scam. I can only wish I had been aware of these tools years before. Ms. Wagner is a gifted writer. I hope she continues to share her experiences in the future."

- Judith Cooper
January 17, 2019

"This book is a very good read. Lots of good advice concerning grief and "pulling yourself up again to start all over." It has a lot of good advice for online dating (or any kind of dating). Shelby is a very interesting and talented writer!"

- Linda Rehmeyer
Music Teacher, Entertainer

"As a happily married woman of forty-eight years, I found this book to be very enlightening. Several of my friends and relatives are widowed or divorced, and they are starting the dating scene. . .again. This book helped me become aware of their journey through loss, trials, depression, and finally the success of living again and becoming whole. This book covers many

subjects that women of all ages will probably go through at some point in their lives. It is a must read that will help readers understand a woman's journey through life."

- J.K. Davis, author of
"Secrets Best Shared,"
- quilter, teacher, and friend

CONTENTS

BE CAREFUL

This book is dedicated to my family.

*Life
is not about
Waiting for the
Storm
to Pass;
It is about
Learning to Dance
in the Rain.*[1]

–Vivian Greene

FOREWORD

"Shelby's book is inspiring to all women and men. She took a vast subject and divided its complexities into individual sections. It is relatable, intellectual, and investigative. Wagner starts her book as a broken woman and ends a strong one. Her journey through the toils of online dating is eye opening and will be helpful to everyone out there trying to find 'the one'. This book is both a self-help guide and a genius approach to conquering romance scammers. Much like a profiler, she brings the essence of a sleuth examining the mysterious men of the internet. Do they want you for you? Are they preying on you? Are they after your money and nothing more? Shelby takes her readers on a ride they won't soon forget."

Samantha Stone, Events Coordinator/ Volunteer Facilitator/ Activities Coordinator St Joseph County Commission on Aging. August 23, 2018.

ACKNOWLEDGEMENTS

Many thanks to my family and to my dear friends Josie Briggs, Judy Cooper, June Davis, John Day, Ken Kooiman, Janet Hutchins, William Milton, Samantha Stone, and Patty Wolff-Wagner. I thank you very much for your help, support, encouragement, and patience with me during this time; for listening when I needed a friendly ear; for giving advice whenever I asked for it; and for taking the time to proof my manuscript. I really appreciate each and everyone of you.

INTRODUCTION

[NOTE: Due to popular demand, this book is an expanded and updated version of my first book, "Learning to Dance in the Rain - Dealing with Grief, Moving On and Online Dating," released December 19, 2018.]

The loss of a spouse is *the* most stressful event in one's life. In fact, when my husband suddenly passed away in 2016, I was devastated! Since I had married a man eight years older than I was, I knew it was a strong possibility that I would outlive him. I refused to think about it, however, telling myself I would deal with it when (and if) it happened. Fast forward fifty years and suddenly, it was no longer a possibility, but my reality. I had become a widow! Stunned, I had no idea how I was going to survive this terrible tragedy! Luckily, I had two supportive adult children who helped me get through the ordeal.

I have told my story in four sections. In part 1, the story begins with my husband's last four days alive and the events immediately following his passing. It continues with my grieving and transition through the grief stages and into the unknowns as I share information and activities I found helpful in my survival. Part 1 is about helping those who are grieving by reminding them to take the time to grieve because it is through grieving that we are healed. It is through healing that we are able to survive the widowhood effect and become enabled to take back our lives and continue living.

Part 4 is a survival guide for internet dating and educates about avoiding the snares of romance scammers.

"A romance scam is a confidence trick involving feigning romantic intentions towards a victim, gaining their affection, and then using that goodwill to commit fraud. Fraudulent acts may involve access to the victim's money, bank accounts, credit cards, passports, e- mail accounts, or national identification numbers; or forcing the victims to commit financial fraud on their behalf. In many instances, a mail-order bride scam will also bait the victim into committing felonies to establish citizenship for the perpetrator."[2] (https://en.wikipedia.org/wiki/Online_romance_scams)

During my journey of grief, I fell victim to a romance scammer, and I admit the damage was a lot more than the loss of the money. I didn't even like the guy, so my heart was not broken in that respect, but I knew better and still sent the money, thinking he would pay me back as he promised. Scammers are masters at manipulation and lies and no one can be certain that it will "never happen to them." I certainly hoped that no one would ever find out what I had done! I did not plan to tell a soul. I was angry enough at myself for being so gullible, and totally humiliated when I finally had to admit what I had done. However, when I learned that I had lots of company and that they had lost even more than I had, I decided to help others make the wiser choice and stick to it. Do not send money (or gifts) to a stranger on the internet, until you have met in person many times and can verify unequivocally that they are deserving of your trust!

In part 2 I share information on a variety of issues I found interesting and helpful as I transitioned through my period of grieving and pursuit of a new lifestyle. Part 3 is an introduction to internet dating with the good and bad.

I chose, "Learning to Dance in the Rain" as the title of my book, because the phrase reminds me to always look to the bright side, stay positive, be active, and it tells of my activity during the worst time of my life, learned to dance.

PART ONE

The Rain

CHAPTER ONE

The Catastrophic Event

In January 2000, my husband, Bob, and I retired and moved to Tennessee to begin building our retirement dream home in the country. Our new house was a Deltec home with seventeen sides. It was circular in design and had no supporting interior walls, which enabled us to design our own unique floor plan and showcase the beautiful panoramic view of the Smoky Mountains.

We were excited to retire and start enjoying the "golden years" we had heard about. We felt blessed. We had lived a good life and expected retirement to be the same. But in late September 2006, we learned Bob had cancer, and the downhill battle began. The ten years that followed were challenging for him as he endured surgery, radiation, hormone therapy, new medications, and treatments.

In June of 2016, we made our annual motor trip to Michigan to visit relatives. While we were at our daughter's home, she offered to drive us to the Upper Peninsula to see my sister and my mother, who was in a nursing home there. I spent most of my time with my mother while Bob enjoyed discussing the Bible and politics with our brother-in-law and babysitting our two-year-old grandson. We all enjoyed the visit, but it was soon time to head South. A few minutes after we were on our way, I became concerned because Bob was coughing a lot, and it didn't sound good. I finally announced my concern, and he retorted that he was fine. Over the next five hours in the car it became more and more evident that he was not fine! However, when I suggested again that he needed to see a doctor before we left for Tennessee, he adamantly refused, declaring that he was not sick and just wanted to get home!

We started for Tennessee as planned early the next morning, but as the miles sped by, the cough became worse and worse, and I considered stopping at a hospital somewhere along the way. Bob kept insisting that he wasn't sick and wanted to go straight home. When we got there, he went straight to his room, saying he would see me in the morning, and we would go out to breakfast.

By morning, he had changed his mind. He just wanted to stay in bed all day. At about 3:00 p.m., he called for me to come to his room. His voice sounded awful, so I set aside the book I was reading and immediately rushed to his room. When I got there, he was huddled under the blanket and told me he was in trouble. He was so weak he was unable to sit up. Assessing the situation, I suggested calling 911, but he didn't want me to. He told me to help him get up and get dressed, and I would take him to the hospital myself. I gathered a shirt and pants, and putting my arms around his shoulders, I pulled him to almost a sitting position and helped him to get dressed. Then I found my walker, and he slid onto it, and I rolled him out to the car.

When we arrived at the emergency entrance of the hospital, I jumped out of the car and ran inside to get help. An attendant followed me out to the car with a wheelchair, and when I told her he couldn't get out alone, she moved in closer and helped him into the chair. Then she pushed him into triage where they recognized he was in trouble and took him straight to the emergency room and helped him onto a bed.

A doctor came to see him almost immediately and ordered x-rays and blood work. We had arrived at the hospital at 5:00 p.m., and at 7:00 p.m., we were told he had pneumonia and would be admitted to the hospital as soon as a room became available. Bob fell asleep as we waited in the emergency room, and I alternately paced the floor and fidgeted on a folding chair. At 10:00 p.m., the attendants came, and I followed as they rolled him out of the emergency room and up the elevator. I thought he would be taken to intensive care, but instead his room was on a regular floor. That surprised me, and I began to think he wasn't as ill as I had thought.

A nurse immediately came to hook him up to the machines, and Bob asked her for some food, insisting that he was very hungry and needed something to eat She responded that he had to wait until after the intubation procedure had been done. Grumbling, Bob settled down and fell asleep again for a short time. By midnight, he no longer had a fever, and his other vitals had returned to normal.

I tried to make myself comfortable, thinking I would stay with him all night, but the room was cold, and I was freezing. I was dressed for a hot summer day and had forgotten to grab a sweater in the rush to leave. The chair in his room was most uncomfortable, and every time I dozed off for a moment, Bob would ask me for something. I was exhausted since I had not slept much the previous four nights worrying about him, and I had just driven five hundred miles to get us home. I was beginning to feel ill myself. I needed to get some sleep soon, or I was going to collapse and be unable to care for him when we got home.

I finally discussed the situation with Bob, who told me to go home. I felt bad about leaving him there, but he was being cared for by nurses, I thought, and I needed to rest. There seemed to be no place for me to rest in the hospital, so I kissed Bob good night and left. It was 1:00 a.m., and I had a forty-five-minute drive home alone which caused me to feel anxious. When I arrived at home, I lay down on my bed and fell asleep as soon as my head hit the pillow.

I awoke suddenly at 6:30 a.m. and called the nurses' station. When there was no answer, I knew I had to get back to the hospital. When I arrived, I found an extremely agitated and distressed husband, who yelled at me to get him some food. His last words to me were, "I'm not going to make it out of this hospital alive!"

I hurried out of his room to look for a nurse, but there was no one in sight. I waited for a few minutes, unsure of what to do next. When a nurse came out of another patient's room, I hurried to catch up with her. I told her my husband was starving and asked why he had not been fed all night. She replied they were still waiting for the intubation procedure to be done. "You mean it hasn't been done yet? They ordered it at eight last night!" I blurted out, stunned.

She shrugged her shoulders and said that she didn't know. I started back to Bob's room, then turned toward the nurse and asked her to tell me again why the procedure was needed. She explained that Bob's rapid, shallow breathing was preventing the medicine from getting where it needed to be. The tube would help the medicine get into his lungs. "He will not get better without it," she concluded.

I returned to Bob's room and was trying to explain the situation to him when the room suddenly filled up with several nurses and two doctors. They were chattering softly among themselves, straightening the sheets and bedclothes, trying to look busy, I thought. Suddenly, the machines were unhooked from the wall, one nurse grabbed the IV stand, and without a word to Bob or myself, they rushed him out of the room. I quickly grabbed my purse and hurried to catch up with them so I would not lose him. A nurse finally noticed me and leaned over to tell me they were taking him to intensive care, and I could not go with them. As we passed a room, she told me to wait there until they got him settled. I asked her how long that would take and was told about fifteen minutes. Then they disappeared through some double doors, and I entered the waiting room and sat down to wait. Fifteen minutes came and went, and I waited, and I waited some more.

Finally, two nurses appeared at the door to the waiting room and motioned for me to come out into the hall. There they quietly told me, "We are sorry to tell you, Mrs. Wagner, but Mr. Wagner didn't make it."

Confused, I asked, "What? What do you mean he didn't make it?"

They reported that they had been trying to insert the tube for the intubation procedure into his throat when his heart stopped, and they had been unable to start it again.

"But you must do something!" I cried.

"There is nothing we can do," they replied. "He is gone."

"No, that can't be true!" I exclaimed.

"Yes," they assured me again. "He is gone! His heart stopped, and we couldn't get it started again!"

"He is gone?" echoed inside of my head. *"But that is impossible! How? Why? I didn't even say goodbye!"*

This scene was embedded in my brain forever, a continuously running replay that was just as painful each time as it had been the first time.

When I remembered that it was I who had signed the paper giving permission for this procedure, I felt like a baseball bat had hit me. *"Oh my god! I had killed my husband. I had signed the paper, and now he was gone! Dead? How can this be? I had killed my husband!*

"Oh, Bob! What have I done? I am so sorry." I moaned.

How could this have happened? What could I have done differently? I remembered every detail of the night before and the many times we had rushed to the hospital over the years. Every time, he had come home with me. How could this time be different?

I remembered his last words—"I'm not going to make it out of this hospital alive!"

Did he know what was going to happen? Why had he said those words? I knew he was frustrated and hungry, but did he know he wasn't going to make it this time? I would never know. I had argued with him right to the end, telling him to resist and encouraging him to hang on. I concluded that I had killed him!

I was crushed with guilt as the "whys" and "shouldas" and "couldas" exploded inside my brain.

Why didn't I take him to the hospital earlier?

Why didn't I call 911?

Why did I agree to the intubation?

How could he go without saying goodbye?

This wasn't supposed to happen!

How could God do this to me?

What on earth do I do now?

How am I going to survive without him?

I prayed silently, *"Dear God, please help me! I don't know what I am going to do. Please let this be a mistake. I need him!"* But I already knew God's answer! He wasn't coming back.

In tears, I collapsed into the waiting arms of my pastor, who had arrived with a fellow parishioner only a few minutes before. "He is gone!" I told them as we embraced and huddled together and my pastor began to pray for Bob, our kids, and me.

When I had gained back some of my composure, I asked my pastor, "So what do I do next?"

He told me the coroner would be coming soon to talk with me. All I had to do was wait. After a few minutes, he asked, "Do you want me to call David and Robin [my son and daughter]?"

Oh my! Our children had to be told! I nodded as I gave him their cell phone numbers. Then I asked him to call my sister. After that, we sat, solemnly waiting for the coroner to come.

When the coroner came, I answered his questions, and he filled out his form. When he was finished, he showed me where I had to sign it. Then I asked him what I should do next. He said that the funeral director would send someone to pick up the body and take it to the funeral home to prepare it for burial and that I would be called to make an appointment the next morning to come to the funeral home and make the funeral arrangements. In the meantime, he suggested that I wait at the hospital for my son, David, and then all of us would be able to go into Bob's room and say our goodbyes.

David was at work in North Carolina, and his wife, Thais, was at work in Johnson City, Tennessee. They both had to find somebody to cover for them before they could leave work. It would take about three hours for them to come. Pastor said he would wait with me for David to arrive so he could talk to him. Afterward, he left us, and as he was leaving, my daughter called to tell me they were on their way from Michigan and would arrive about midnight.

David's wife, Thais, was in her last year of nursing school and had just finished an assignment working in the intensive care unit at a hospital in Johnson City. She had taken care of many terminal patients during this stint and wanted to take care of Bob's body. At first, she was told it was against hospital policy; they later allowed her to do what had to be done when there was an emergency in the ICU. When she had finished, she came to get us and took us to see him. He looked like he was sleeping peacefully. I kissed his forehead and told him I loved him and said goodbye.

We all finally said our goodbyes and decided to go home. I began gathering our things, and as I put Bob's clothes and shoes in a bag, I still could not believe he wasn't going home with me this time. I was in a daze, a fog, and I felt numb. In the blink of an eye, the life I had known for fifty years was gone and I didn't know what I was going to do now. I was alone, and already I missed him.

I kept repeating to myself, *"Oh, Bob! I am so sorry!"*

Later, when David and I were alone, he asked me, "Mom, why do you keep saying that?"

"Because I feel so bad! I am so sorry! This is all my fault! I killed him!" I replied.

"No, Mom, you did not kill him! You did exactly what he wanted."

I knew he was speaking the truth, but it did not make me feel any better.

When we got home, I went to my bedroom and lay down on my bed. I was exhausted, but I could not sleep. Scenes from the hospital played themselves over and over, and I could not stop crying.

"What was I going to do now?" I wondered but had no answer.

A short while later, my son came into my bedroom to tell me he needed to take his family home to North Carolina. He explained they had come straight to the hospital from work and now needed to retrieve his wife's car, and to go home and pack some clothes for the next few days. He said they would come back in the morning for the meeting with the funeral home director. He suggested I call a friend to come over and stay with me until my daughter, Robin, would arrive. I told him I would be alright by myself for that short time, but he wanted me not to be alone. So I called Marilou and she came right over. We talked for a little while after she arrived, but then I finally fell asleep. When my daughter arrived with her family, I heard them and went to greet them. Marilou left, and we went straight to bed. The kids were exhausted from their ten- hour drive.

CHAPTER TWO

First Steps

At nine o'clock the next morning, we met David at the funeral home for our last viewing before the cremation. When we were finished, we were led to a conference room where we discussed the next steps with the director of the funeral home.

1. The fees for the cremation and services performed by the funeral home.
2. When and where the funeral service and visitations would be held.
3. When the ashes would be ready for a family member to pick up. Since he was being cremated, they would not be attending the funeral service.
4. The obituary for their website and the local newspaper.
5. Flower arrangements.
6. Public notice of the funeral service and time.

Because the body was to be cremated, the director told us that the funeral service could take place at any time in the future. However, the immediate family was present already, and others were on their way from Michigan and Colorado. Bob's name had already been placed on a sign in front of the funeral home to inform our local friends, and our pastor had utilized our direct call system to inform parishioners, so we decided to have the service in two days, which would be Thursday at 11:00 a.m. preceded by a single viewing at 10:00 a.m.

When we got home, I posted the news on my Facebook page and began to plan the funeral service. I was the church secretary, and one of my responsibilities was to prepare a printed program for all funeral services in the church, so I set about working on the one for my husband. Robin began to prepare a display of family photos while David and his uncle went to prepare the grave site at the church cemetery, and my son-in-law began preparing a meal for all of us.

I knew the word had gotten out when friends and neighbors started to call to express their condolences and to stop by with food for us. They were very thoughtful, and I was grateful for their support. Since we had lived there only seventeen years, I thought it was amazing that we had made so many friends.

Bob would have been pleased to see all the people who came to the church for his funeral. The building was nearly full. At 10:00 a.m., the line of people began to fill and by 10:30, it stretched from the front of the church all the way back the aisle to the church's entrance. It was a busy hour as friends shook my hand and hugged me and said all the right words. Only twice did I have a chance to look up at the line. When I did, I was pleased to see the crowd and surprised when I saw one of my cousins who lived in Knoxville, and another from Arkansas. They had seen my post on Facebook and had come to honor Bob. Thank God for technology!

I was pleased with the display of photos on two computers at the front of the church and the arrangement of the beautiful walnut box with praying hands that contained Bob's ashes with a vase of flowers on one side and a photo of Bob as a young man on the other. Everything looked very nice. I know the friends enjoyed out family photos. I overheard one of them say, "Oh my! Bob was a very handsome young man!" I smiled and nodded as I responded, "I always thought so."

It was a shame that none of Bob's extended family could make it because of age and travel distance. His only sister was in the hospital fighting for her life at the time, but I knew she really wanted to be there. She did send me an email in which she told some of the memories of her older brother, whose responsibility was to take care of her when she was little and their parents were at work. My sister read the email aloud during the service.

I chose Bob's favorite hymn, "The Lord of the Dance." He liked its catchy Shaker tune and that the words of the hymn told the complete story of Jesus' lfe. I chose the second hymn, "It is Well with My Soul," because I knew Bob's soul was with God. The third hymn, "The Borning Cry," was unfamiliar to my family, the local members knew the tune, and it was appropriate. The words were comforting because they reminded everyone that God is always with us; at our birth and at our end, and everything in between.

Pastor Deal led the service, and two of our dear Parrottsville friends provided the music on the piano and flute. My brother-in-law provided some of his memories, causing us to smile at his humor, and my sister also shared some of her memories of Bob. Somehow, we got through it all, even though it was difficult. Pastor Deal told me he had counted eighty-five people who had stayed for the wonderful lunch prepared by our church families, and I knew there were several people who could not stay.

David's two best friends surprised him by their attendance. One had come from Charlotte, North Carolina, and the other from Nashville, Tennessee. I really appreciated their being present for my son because he really needed their support and thoughtfulness. He was in a tough spot and was touched that they had come. We invited them to follow us home after the service and they were a big help in our transition from all the activity of the past few days.

I collapsed into my recliner and fell asleep with the comforting sound of friendly voices and laughter filling the air. When I awoke about an hour later, it was so quiet, I assumed everyone had left. Opening my eyes, I found everybody sitting quietly in a circle in front of me, as if I was center stage. I immediately suspected something was up, and I was right! When I moved my hand, it brushed against something hard in my lap, and looking down, I saw my lap was full of empty beer bottles and a wine bottle.

"What is this?" I asked suspiciously.

A voice from the crowd replied, "You'd better be good, or we are going to post this photo on Facebook!"

"Very funny!" I exclaimed, and we all had a good laugh. It felt good to laugh, and the laughter sounded wonderful.

Once the company had left, my family disappeared to their own rooms to rest and I was alone with my uncertain future. What was I going to do now? What did I want to do? How was I going to manage? I had some difficult decisions to make. I wanted to stay in my home in Tennessee, but none of my family lived nearby and I was afraid to live there by myself because the neighbors were quite far up the hill. Another issue was the fact that my husband and I had designed and built the house and I wasn't sure I could live there alone with my memories. In addition, I had a large mortgage payment and I wasn't sure I could pay it with my newly reduced income.

That evening, my daughter and her husband offered a solution and, after discussing the details with her brother, we all agreed that I should accept it. Her suggestion was for me to move back to Michigan where I would live with them until my Tennessee house sold. That would give me time to grieve and to consider what I wanted to do with the rest of my life.

Once the decision to return to Michigan was made, we began to make plans and to pack up the house. We would separate everything into what I would need for a Michigan winter at my daughter's and what would be moved in the future when the house would have a buyer.

Three weeks after the funeral, my son-in-law arrived with his truck and a trailer. We loaded my things and, within and hour or so, we were on our way North. My daughter told me we would leave my car in my garage and come back for it sometime in the future. In the meantime, she felt we both needed to be in the same car because we were exhausted and needed each other to stay awake. When we arrived at their house, my son-in-law was already unloading the truck. About an hour later, his sister and her family arrived to help and within a very short time, I was established in my new home.

[Since then, I have met several widows whose families were not nearly as supportive as mine, and I have come to realize how blessed I am. I will always be very grateful to my daughter and her husband for their hospitality and loving support. They made me feel welcome and comfortable during the eight months I lived with them.]

We all grieved in different ways. I missed my husband, and I cried a lot whenever I was alone. I talked to God, praying that all I had believed about heaven was true and that Bob was really there. During the days, the kids were away at work, and I was alone. Used to my husband being around all the time, I was lonely, and I missed him. I even asked God why he had not taken me too.

I have always believed God has a plan for each of us, and we need to be patient while we wait for him to reveal that plan. In the meantime, I had the privilege of watching my only grandchild grow from a two-year-old toddler into a four-year-old grown-up. *Wow!* What an experience that was!

CHAPTER THREE

Grieving is Necessary

What is grief? What does it mean to grieve? Why is it necessary to do so? The root word is *grief.* According to Wikipedia,

> "Grief is the response to loss, particularly to the loss of someone that has died, to which a bond or affection was formed . . . Grieving is painful, personal, and normal. To grieve is to experience grief, to feel deep sorrow. Grieving has physical, cognitive, behavioral, social, cultural, spiritual and philosophical dimensions. Synonyms of grief are sorrow, misery, sadness, heartache, heartbreak . . ."[1]

Why does the death of a spouse top the list as the most stressful event in one's life? Why is there a widowhood effect, the title given to the statistic that many surviving spouses pass away within this first three months to a year following the first? Why is it important to allow time to grieve?

I think my story as told in chapters 1 and 2 explains how catastrophic the loss of my husband was to me. Therefore, in this chapter I will discuss the third question—why is grieving important and necessary, and offer some suggestions that helped me to avoid that widowhood effect.

Grieving is healing. We cannot heal without it. It is during the process of grieving that we come to terms with our loss and make sense of our new reality as a single person. The passage of time helps to ease our pain, and we need to give ourselves this time.

Some people refuse to allow themselves to grieve, ashamed to let others see their pain. They may fill their lives with activity, thinking they are too busy or that they don't need to show their emotions. Some people, men especially, think they must appear to be strong so they hide their feelings. If you are reading this right now and are guilty of thinking like this, please stop. Know that it is normal to feel sad whenever we lose someone we love. It is normal to say goodbye, and it is OK to allow yourself to feel the emotions you are feeling. If you need someone to give you permission to feel sad, then I give it to you right now. Know that it is normal to feel sad and to grieve.

Even animals grieve when someone they love leaves them, whether it is an adult or even another animal. My daughter had two German Shepherds, and when Abby (the oldest one) died, Jewels, the survivor, was listless and sad. She would go to Abby's favorite places, sniff around, and whine as if to ask, "Where is Abby?" Jewels missed her friend and could not understand what had happened to her. If animals can grieve, then you can also. You have my permission. It is alright.

Grief has many faces. It has no set rules or time limits. Each person must grieve in his or her own way. According to Earl A. Grollman, a certified death educator and counselor who was cited as "Hero of the Heartland" for his work with the families and volunteers of the Oklahoma City bombing, "Grief is not a disorder, a disease, or a sign of weakness. It is an emotional, physical, and spiritual necessity; the price you pay for love. The only cure for grief is to grieve."[2]

Pay attention to that last sentence for it is important! Ponder it for a moment. One must grieve in order to heal.

One friend told me, "But I don't want to heal." That is OK. There is nothing wrong with this statement. However, at some point, you will be ready to stop feeling sad all the time. At least I hope you will. We must not live in the past. I read somewhere that the past is a reference point not a dwelling place. We live. We learn from our past. We die. We grieve. We pick up the pieces of our lives, put them back together again, and get on with living. It is a process, and we must move on.

Grollman says, "Each person's grief journey is as unique as a fingerprint or a snowflake."[3] In other words, each of us grieves in our own way. Our friends and relatives need to respect our differences. We may not do the same things they do when they feel sad, but that doesn't mean what we do is wrong, nor does it mean what they do is wrong. It just means we are different from one another, and that is the way it is. Everyone must learn to be patient and considerate of those who are grieving. This is not the place for criticism. This is the place for support. We need a friend who is willing to give us attention, someone who just listens whenever we feel like talking.

I particularly liked the explanations given by Darby Faubion regarding the seven stages of grief. She lists them like this: (1) Shock and Denial, (2) Guilt and Pain, (3) Anger and Bargaining, (4) Depression, Reflection and Loneliness, (5) the Upward Turn, (6) Reconstruction and Working, and (7) Acceptance and Hope.[4] (www.regain.us/advice)

I reacted with shock and denial when the nurse said to me, "He didn't make it." I didn't understand what she meant, and I responded hesitantly, "What did you say?" After repeating the phrase, she added, "His heart couldn't take the procedure, and it stopped." I immediately responded, "No! You must do something!" I accused, "No! You are wrong!"

How could I have reacted any differently? I had not expected him to die! This was catastrophic news, and I was devastated. How could this happen?

When the ugly thought that I had killed my husband by signing the paper giving permission popped into my mind, I immediately concluded that I was guilty, and immediately I prayed, *"No, please, God, let it not be true!"*

I was in shock. I blamed myself and thought I was guilty. I remembered painfully that I should have insisted he go to the doctor sooner! I should have called an ambulance. I didn't have the chance to say goodbye to him or to tell him once more that I loved him. I was stunned and in deep distress. The tears flooded my eyes and spilled down my face.

Then I became *angry*. I was angry because he had left me without saying goodbye, and angry that he had left me alone to deal with the rest of my life. Angrily, I cried out, "How dare you leave me to deal with this alone!" I hissed into the air. "How could you do this to me?"

My life became very busy and the initial shock wore off. My family arrived and there was so much to do.

First there was the funeral service to plan. After the funeral, I became entrenched in packing for my relocation to Michigan. I was so busy I hardly noticed the tears rolling down my cheeks. I could not sleep. I could not eat and I lost ten pounds. I forgot to take my medicines. I chastised myself for not having been a better wife, for not having taken better care of him.

Acceptance? Hope? How can we accept our spouse's death? We accept gifts. We accept the kind words people say to us. We accept help when offered. How can we accept that someone we love as been taken from us? It is expected that we will say, "Thank you," when we accept something. Am I supposed to say, "Thank you for taking my husband?" or "It is alright that he is gone."

"Never!" I say. "Never will I accept his death! Yes, he was gone, but I will never accept it!"

I did not want to accept the fact that he was dead. However, slowly I got used to being alone. Slowly I began to pick up the pieces of my life and put them back together again, not as my life had been but as a new, completely new life alone. Slowly I began to hope for something more.

I still feel his presence. We had started a web design business soon after our retirement and we worked side by side with out desks next to each other so we could easily discuss our ideas. I have been alone two years now and every once in a while, I get an idea, and I think, *Oh, I must show this to Bob!* Then I remember . . .

Sometimes I see something flit by my eye and I look up, but can see nothing. I wonder, *"Is Bob checking in on me?"* It seemed as if I had a ghost in my house. When I mentioned this to my aunt, she admitted a similar experience. She then shared with me that every Sunday morning as she sat with her coffee looking out a window, a red cardinal would appear on the bush just outside. She said she thought it was her deceased husband paying her a visit as in the traditional story of a red cardinal. I was unfamiliar with this story so I looked it up on the internet and learned that the red cardinal is a symbol of death and its appearance represents a visit from a deceased loved one.[5] I then recalled having seen a red cardinal near my windows on several occasions and now whenever I see one, I think of my husband and both my parents who are also deceased. Here is the poem, "Cardinal Spirit", by Janis Leslie Evans for whom the cardinal reminded her of her mother.

> Perched in front of my house Dressed in your favorite color
> You greeted me with your spirit "Welcome Back!"
> You appeared to let me know "I am with you."
>
> I see you in the morning Flying through the air
> Landing on the porch roof Or perching on a branch of a tree
> High in the sky, swooping downward You stop in your tracks
> Giving pause to your daughter.
>
> Looking out for you, expecting you Knowing you will show
> Keeping your visits of promise Even at mid-afternoon
> As I'm leaving out There you are, waving your wing
> Bidding me, "Have a good day."
>
> My heart still broken Losing you too soon
> Needing to hear your voice Missing our talks and laughs
> The presence of the cardinal Ushering in your spirit
> Comforts my soul.[6]

Sometimes, I think it would be easier to just give up. The simple task of *living* sometimes overwhelms me, and I think it would be better if God would just take me too. I am so lonely and uncertain about things. I am depressed. I have become forgetful of late. I forget to eat, and I forget what day it is. Yes, I am tired of feeling sad all the time.

How is it that once something is gone, we appreciate it more than when we had it? I now remember all the little things my husband used to do for me, and I wonder if I thanked him for doing them. Did he know how much I appreciated what he did for me and with me? I miss him, and I feel sad he is not with me anymore.

Sometimes I feel that the struggle to survive is just too difficult, that it would be easier to just give up. Every once in a while, I hear that a surviving spouse passed away not long after the first, and I wonder if they just gave up because it had become too difficult to live alone. I searched the internet and learned that there is a name for this phenomenon. It is called the Widowhood Effect and statistics show that widows and widowers have a 66 percent increased chance of dying within the first three to six months after their spouse. I understand. I "get it." The loneliness is at times unbearable, but I am a survivor. There is something inside of me that keeps pushing me forward.

Yes, I am still grieving, but I am OK. I guess I am on the road to my healing. How about you? I hope you are moving forward as well. I know that I will never get over the loss of my beloved husband and, although time is supposed to make things easier, I wonder, "*When, Lord? When will I feel better? When will this get easier?*"

Tears still roll slowly down my cheeks, and at other times, it is as if a tsunami has hit me as I am overcome with tears and sobbing. A song on the radio fills me with sadness and my whole body starts shaking. One minute I am fine, and the next I am a mess.

Crying does help me to feel better. I am an emotional person anyway. I cry at weddings and funerals and movies. My husband once asked me why I continued to watch a movie that made me cry. My response was, "Because it is a good movie." He never understood.

Please don't be ashamed to cry. It does help. Crying brings relief. My sister told me that she believes God gave us tears to wash away our sadness. He gave us tears to clean our eyes, and maybe he also gave us tears to wash away our sadness. I can accept that.

Tears are mentioned in the Bible at least a hundred times. In Revelations 21:4, when John talks about heaven, he wrote, "And God shall wipe away all tears from their eyes; and there shall be no more death, neither sorrow, nor crying, neither shall there be any more pain: for the former things are passed away."[7]

"No more pain . . ." That would be wonderful, wouldn't it? To a person whose pain is almost unbearable, I believe heaven would be a welcome relief. Do you believe your loved ones are in heaven? Do you believe they are no longer in pain? If they are in a better place with no pain or suffering, then are they not better off there? Why would we want them to come back to their suffering and pain? That would be selfish, wouldn't it? I believe my loved ones are in heaven, and that is the best place for them. Yes, I miss them, but I would not want them to come back to a painful life just because I selfishly wanted them back.

When my neighbor dropped off some cinnamon rolls she had made, she asked if I would like to read a small brochure about death and dying that she had brought with her. I told her that I would like to read it and so she gave it to me. I have read one of the articles over many times as its message is a good one to remember. In it the author compares our body to the shell of an egg, and our souls to the yolk. The shell is fragile, and when it breaks, the yolk is set free. Likewise, when our body dies, our soul is set free. We are set free—free of our pain, free of our burdens, free to be happy, free!

I know my loved ones are in heaven, for they accepted Jesus Christ as their Lord and Savior many years ago and lived to serve him. They accepted his grace and lived as they thought he wanted them to live. They lived long and fruitful lives, and when their bodies wore out, Jesus set them free. I believe he will set me free also one of these days. How about you?

What do you believe? If you believe your loved ones are in heaven, then believe in the fact that they are free from pain. Believe they are happy, and they want you to be happy as well. They do not want you to live in the past. They want you to live in the present and to live your life to the fullest. I keep reminding myself that the past is a source of reference, not a dwelling place! You may want to remember it also.

I am convinced that God wants us to live each day as it comes and, not only that, but that he wants us to be happy. My friend, John, told me once that we should do at least one thing every day to help someone feel better. That will make every day a good day.

I believe that if we want to find a new partner, then God is in favor of it. I miss the companionship of a partner, and I hope and pray that God will help me find someone new with whom to share the rest of my life. I believe that the verse in Genesis 2:18 which reads, "God did not mean for man to live alone," [8] is also true when we are in our senior years. Even our wedding vows which include the words, *until death do us part*, obviously releases us from that marriage commitment and frees us to marry someone else, if we so choose. God has given us freedom to move on.

CHAPTER FOUR

Getting Back to The Business of Living

When a member of one's family dies, everyone is affected and each person grieves in his/her own way. It is an extremely stressful time for all concerned. Each person in the family needs to be considerate and supportive of all others. This is not the time to air past grievances with one another, nor is it the time for arguments. Discussions need to be discussed calmly with consideration given to each member's opinion. Hopefully, all family members can set aside petty annoyances or past hurt feelings with siblings so that the decisions made are best for the surviving spouse. There is no room for selfishness here. Unfortunately, many families fall apart during this time instead of pulling together for the greater good of the family. All members must remain calm and considerate of others, offering their help wherever it may be needed.

Here is a checklist of things to be done immediately:

- Notify all family members and friends;
- Make the burial and funeral arrangements;
- Change account information at banks and other businesses (if necessary);
- Schedule appointments with an attorney for the reading of the will, etc.

Other issues that may have to be discussed after the funeral service is over:

- Will the family home have to be sold?
- Where will the surviving spouse live?
- Will he or she have to relocate?
- What belongings will need to be sold or donated?
- Helping hands will be needed to pack and move if a relocation is imminent.
- A surviving spouse may need help setting up a new budget due to a reduced income.

Change is always difficult, and it is even more difficult at a time like this. It is necessary for all family members to be patient and cautious and to use good judgment. Each person needs to focus on the things that must be done and offer their assistance.

If possible, it is a good thing to remember something I read many years ago that a surviving spouse should make no major decisions, like selling a house or relocating, within the first year after a spouse dies. However, in my case, we had been trying to sell our house for several years prior to his passing so I just continued with the agreement we had made earlier.

Six months after my relocation, I received an offer for my Tennessee house and began looking for one to buy in Michigan. As it turned out, I bought the house in Michigan on a Wednesday, and sold the one in Tennessee the following Friday. I had to wait a month before I could move into the one in Michigan so I returned to Tennessee to vacate that house and then had to put my furniture and other belongings into storage near my new home.

By the time I moved into the new house, I had already familiarized myself with my new community. I had located a senior center nearby and after the move, I began eating lunch there so that I could meet people and make some new friends. I signed up for line dance classes because I had always thought I would like to learn how to do that and because I needed the exercise. I also began playing cards there twice a week and I volunteered to play the piano at lunch time once a week.

Although there were days when I really didn't feel like going out, I knew it was important and so I made myself go. I suggest that you start working on a bucket list of activities you think sound interesting and fun, then choose one and get started having fun with other adults as soon as possible.

Babysitting your grandkids may be fun occasionally and helpful to their parents, but do you really want to babysit them all the time? Think about it. You raised your kids and now it is your time to have some fun. Look around you and talk to other adults and find out what is available in your local area. The activities you choose to do become your "dances." You might want to consider volunteering your services or teaching others a skill you have. Learn a new hobby. Begin to socialize again and to have fun.

If you need help in deciding what you would like to do, start brainstorming. Make a list of at least twenty-five activities that you think might be interesting and fun. That will be your "bucket list." Choose at least three of them and get started right now.

I discovered single's dances were held every weekend and I decided to go to one. I had to drive thirty minutes to an hour by myself to get there and I was scared the first time I went. I was in unfamiliar territory and didn't know anybody. I almost backed out, but I finally gathered up my courage and went. There were over a hundred people there and at first no one talked to me. I was alone, but I stuck it out. After sitting by myself for about an hour, I was bored and thought about going home. But then I told myself I had three options: (1) I could go home and feel sorry for myself; (2) I could continue sitting there alone and feel sorry for myself; or (3) I could ask a man to dance with me and see what would happen.

I put a smile on my face, walked across the room to where a man was sitting alone near the door, and asked if he had come to dance. He said, "Yes." That was the beginning of my metamorphosis. We introduced ourselves and he asked where I was from. When I told him, I had just moved to Sturgis, he pointed out two ladies he knew lived there. When the song ended, I thanked him and went over to the table he had pointed out and introduced myself. Right away, one of the ladies told me to get my coat and purse and come sit with them. I began having fun that night and have since become friends with many of the regulars. I think dancing is a lot of fun, and it is good exercise.

Other activities or "dances" I enjoy are the following: playing euchre (twice a week), hand and foot canasta (once a week), line dancing, directing church choirs, playing the piano at the senior center and nursing homes, and traveling. I have taken the following senior bus trips alone and with some of my new friends: a musical in Chicago; the Shakespeare Festival in Stratford, Ontario; the Creation Museum in Ohio and Noah's Ark in Kentucky, and down the Mississippi River on a Steamboat from Dubuque, Iowa, to Moline, Illinois. I have even traveled alone to North Carolina, Colorado, Montana, and upper Michigan.

Here is a listing of my other "dances" or activities:

1. Join a grief support group if you have not gotten involved in one. It is good therapy to talk with others who are going through the same thing you are. Check out groups that may be sponsored by a local church, local hospital, or senior centers.
2. Keep in touch with your family or friends. Perhaps you do not know what to say, and vice versa, but that is OK. Just call them and say hello.

    Or maybe you could give a copy of this anonymous letter to your friends and family to help them better understand how to help you:

    > Please be gentle with me, for I am grieving. The sea I swim in is a lonely one, and the shore seems miles away. Waves of despair numb my soul as I struggle through each day. My heart is heavy with sorrow. I want to shout and scream and repeatedly ask, "Why?" At times my grief overwhelms me, and I weep bitterly. So great is my loss. Please don't turn away or tell me to move on with my life. I

must embrace my pain before I can begin to heal. Companion me through my tears and sit with me in loving silence. Honor where I am in my journey, not where you think I should be.

Listen patiently to my story. I may need to tell it over and over again. This is how I begin to grasp the enormity of my loss. Nurture me through the weeks and months ahead. Forgive me when I seem distant and inconsolable. A small flame still burns within my heart, and shared memories may trigger both laughter and tears. I need your support and understanding. There is no right or wrong way to grieve. I must find my own path. Please, will you walk beside me? (Anonymous)

3. Please do not be ashamed to cry. It is helpful as I mentioned earlier, and it does bring relief, if only for a short time. It really does.
4. Talk to someone. It could save your life (or theirs). My friend John shared with me that he had been considering suicide three months after his wife passed away. One day, he went to the store and met a friend who exclaimed, "John, you look awful! Come . . . let's get a coke and talk!" John says that friend saved his life!
5. Remember that talking with someone is good therapy and helps both people feel better.
6. Call someone on the phone to chat or go visit them. You will both feel better. I guarantee it! Wouldn't it be awesome to save someone's life by just giving them a chance to talk?
7. Take up your journal and start writing. You can write letters to your deceased loved one telling him/her how you feel about what happened. No one is going to see your journal, so write freely. Tell him/her whatever you feel like saying and what you have been doing since he went away. Tell him/her why you are sad and anything else you feel.

8. If someone hurts your feelings or has irritated you, write down what you would like to say to them in your journal. Don't send it to them or show it to them. Just writing about your feelings is therapeutic. You could write it on a piece of toilet paper and flush it down the drain. Let it go.

9. Sometimes I get stuck thinking about something that is bothering me, and it keeps going around and around in my mind. Does this happen to you? Here is how I have always dealt with this problem. I pray about it, asking God to take care of it for me. This helps for a short while, but hours later I find I am worrying about it again. I don't know why this happens, but it does. I wonder why I took it back. I had asked God to help me with this problem. Did I not believe he would take care of it for me? Friends have told me they do this too. Why do we do this? I don't know, but a few years ago, I found another way to deal with it. I tell myself to *stop regurgitating*!

Where did this come from? I lived in the country in Tennessee, and everywhere we went, we saw cows in the fields doing their "thing." What is their thing? Chewing their cuds, of course. One day, as I saw them in the field chewing their cuds, it suddenly occurred to me that this process is called *regurgitation*. That very day I had been "chewing" on a problem which kept going around and around in my brain and all of a sudden it hit me that I was doing the same thing with my thoughts as the cows were doing with their food. I was regurgitating my thoughts. Perhaps you never thought about this before, but a second definition for the word *regurgitation* is "to repeat a thought without analyzing or comprehending it."[1] Isn't this what I was doing? Perhaps I was trying to analyze the thought, but I wasn't getting anywhere with it.

I decided right then that the next time my mind was stuck thinking in a circle, I would tell myself to *"stop regurgitating!"* It worked! Perhaps you will think it sounds gross . . . but, you get the picture. It works!

10. Several years ago, I spotted a small oval wooden box at a craft show in Gatlinburg. On the top of the lid were wooden letters that read, "My God Box." Inside the lid, was written these words, "When your head starts to worry, and your mind can't rest, put your thoughts on paper, and let God do the rest." I bought the box (this was prior to the regurgitation idea), and whenever I found myself worrying about something or someone, I would write my concern on a piece of paper and put it in the box. That was my way of reminding myself I had prayed about it. Later, when the thought returned, I would remind myself that I had given the problem to God and I wasn't going to worry about it any more. A few months later I would open the box and discover that God had indeed taken care of it for me! The problem had been solved.

11. Here is something to think about. It may sound a little weird, but hey, it's mine! "We need to do the *opposite* of whatever it is that we *feel* like doing. Here's an example, maybe I do not *feel* like smiling at the waitress in the restaurant, but I smile at her anyway. My smile causes her to smile back and now I feel better than I did before, and so does she. Try it sometime and see what happens. Doing something (whether we feel like it or not) usually makes us feel better than sitting doing nothing. Remember, that *something* can be *anything*. Choose any activity).

    I have a friend who says he feels like doing nothing so he sits in his favorite chair all day watching television, then complains he doesn't have any energy. He falls asleep sitting there and wakes up feeling even worse. He can't sleep at night. I told him he needs to do the opposite. He needs to get up out of that chair, get dressed and go somewhere, or take a walk. Start a conversation with someone. In fact, he will feel better. He admits that he feels better after a walk, but getting started is the problem.

12. Here is something to do whenever you feel angry. You will allow yourself ten minutes to feel the anger (or whatever you

are feeling). Set a timer for ten minutes and do whatever you want to do—cry, yell, holler, scream, pound your fists into a pillow, etc. When the timer rings, *stop!* Go take a shower and shave, or put on your makeup, get dressed in something that makes you look and feel good, then get out of the house! Go somewhere—anywhere! Just go!

Smile at everyone you see! Remember, a smile is a free gift you give to someone, and it is usually returned. This makes both the giver and the receiver feel better! Say hello to them and start talking. Don't be shy! That other person is probably just as lonely as you are and glad that someone is talking with him/her. Don't worry that you don't know what to say or that you will say the wrong thing. Just open your mouth and let the words come out. The important thing is that you are talking to somebody! You are having a conversation. It feels good to talk, and it makes the other person feel good too. You have just made a new friend. Isn't that wonderful? Repeat as necessary.

13. Pretend that you are happy, and you will feel happy!
14. Pretend that you are enthusiastic, and you will become enthusiastic!
15. Fake it until you make it!
16. Remember your loved one. Enjoy your memories. Our loved ones are with us forever in our hearts, and it is good to remember them. Allow yourself to feel whatever emotion is evoked by their memory. Our memories are a part of us. We are who we are now because our loved ones were a part of our lives. It is right to remember them. Here are some suggestions to help us remember a loved one:

   • Plant a tree or bush in their memory in a prominent place in your yard.
   • Place a stone or other marker in your garden. Mine is engraved with this phrase: Those we love don't go away. They walk beside us every day.

- At Christmastime, place a chair in his or her memory in a prominent place, or include a Christmas stocking with their name on it on the fireplace.

17. Become active in your church or community and volunteer your time and help.
18. Take a class that will get you moving and out of the house. If there is something you always wanted to do someday. Do it now!
19. Start learning something new—a craft, to dance, play a new card game, or to cook. Get out of your comfort zone and get out of the house.
20. Make a new friend.
21. Teach a skill you have to others.
22. Albert Einstein once said, "We cannot solve our problems with the same thinking we used to create them."[2]
23. Decide to think positively instead of negatively. Our future is determined by the way in which we react to our challenges. We can choose to react negatively or positively. Negativity only makes us feel depressed as well as everyone around us. Why make ourselves feel bad when we can do the opposite? Choose to be positive, and choose to have a good day!
24. Writing your thoughts in your journal will help you to feel better. Keep a list of all the things that make you happy and add something new every day. Then "act" on them.
25. Change your thoughts.
    Change your actions.
    Change yourself.
    Change your life!

CHAPTER FIVE

The Talk

About seven months after I moved in with my daughter, I began to make some decisions about my future. My sister had suggested a few months earlier that I should start thinking about dating again. She suggested I should get married again. I scoffed at the idea, saying I never wanted to get married again! However, with time, I began to change my mind.

However, living in the country meant I was alone most of the day while everyone else was working. I was lonely, and although I had no trouble keeping myself busy, I decided it would be nice to have a friend. Eating alone in a restaurant was extremely difficult, and going shopping by myself was tedious and lonely. Seeing other people in couples talking and enjoying each other's company looked more inviting than an old lady sitting alone.

I enjoyed eating out and going to the movies, but I was lonely and I missed my friends in Tennessee. I decided I needed some new friends. I went to the local senior center and started playing pinochle with a group. The people were alright, but as soon as the games were over, they congregated in groups or hurried out of the room. Some were making plans to get together elsewhere. I was not included so I left. No one even thought about me. They knew I was new in town. These people had been friends a long time and I was the "new kid in town. I felt excluded.

At that time, I had not been informed yet about the singles' dances. Perhaps I should have asked them what other activities they liked, but I was a new widow and very unsure of myself. One day as I was surfing the internet for something of interest, an ad for a dating website popped up. I decided to take a look at it just to check it out. It looked rather confusing, but interesting. I began to wonder what it would be like to actually chat with someone and maybe even meet someone. I decided to talk about it with my daughter before doing anything about it. One evening when we were fixing supper, I started the conversation.

"I've been thinking about signing up for an internet dating website. What would you think about me starting to date again?"

"What?" she snapped at me. "Mom, you don't want to do that!"

"Why not?" I asked. "I am lonely, and I need a friend!"

"How can you be lonely with all the people dropping in here all the time?" she asked.

I responded, "These people are your friends and relatives. They come to see you and your husband, not me. Everyone is friendly enough, and I appreciate that they include me in family events, but you are all busy with your own lives, and when you are working or go out with your friends, I am lonely. I need my own friends, someone to go shopping with or to the movies. I need companionship. I have been here for seven months, and I haven't met anyone I didn't know before your father died. I seem to have gotten lost! I don't even know who I am anymore! How can I figure out what I want to do with the rest of my life when I don't even know who I am? Or what my options are?"

"Why don't you ask Kathy at church? She'll go out to lunch with you, I'm sure!"

"I've already asked her, and she is busy with her family. She is worried about her heart and afraid to get too far from home," I answered.

"Well, you certainly do not need to go on a dating site. Why don't you go back to the senior center? You liked to play cards there, didn't you?"

"Not really. Those people are sharks. They play to win! That isn't any fun! They are all more interested in one another and the cards in their hands than in making a new friend!" I replied.

"Well, I can tell you the men on those dating sites are not looking for a friend! They are not even real! They are out there in cyberspace . . ." she exclaimed as she waved her hands in the air ". . . the netherworld of the internet! They'll tell you anything, promise you the moon, rob you blind! You need to find real, live friends . . . and while you're at it, stick to women friends."

"No one around here seems to want to be my friend!" I insisted. "If I continue doing what I have been doing, I will never meet anyone new. I have to do something different!"

"I just don't think you're ready to start dating again, Mom. Besides, you are still grieving! I think you should wait longer before trying to date again! You don't remember how hard dating is! It was hard enough fifty years ago, and it is even worse now."

Supper was ready, and the conversation ended. After dinner, I went up to my room and called my son. When I told him what I was thinking about doing, he almost exploded! His reaction was even worse than his sister's as he yelled into the phone, "Mom you *do not* want to do that!"

"You met your wife on a dating site," I reminded him.

"That is different!" he insisted. "No, Mom! Don't do it!"

I decided to wait a little longer. A few days later, I registered for my first online dating website. My objective was to make a new a friend.

And I made several new friends, actually.

But along the way, I learned quite a lot about dating and relationships and the dangers lurking in the shadows, and I learned there was a lot that I didn't know.

PART TWO

Learning to Dance

CHAPTER SIX

I Like Myself

With everything that had been going on during the last few months, Shelby (me) had gotten lost. My self-confidence was at zero, and my self-image was a disgrace. I had begun second-guessing myself, and making a decision was difficult. My life had changed. I was no longer somebody's wife. I was no longer a part of a couple. I was no longer the caretaker of a sick husband. I had been catapulted into a new life, without a choice. I had uprooted myself and moved into a new community, far from my old friends. I was alone at seventy-five, insecure, and felt I had lost control of my life.

I was reading a lot, questioning everything and asking myself some difficult questions. I was searching for answers to questions I had not yet asked myself. One thing that bothered me a lot was that I had begun to doubt God. My husband had been a strong influence in this department. He was a Bible scholar, always sharing what he was learning. After he was gone, I began to wonder whether my beliefs were mine because I believed them or because I knew he believed them. Some of the questions I asked myself were the following:

Who am I? What do I stand for? In what do I put my trust? What are my values? Am I the best person I can be? Am I a quality person? Am I making good decisions? Do I know my self-worth? Do I have boundaries, and if I do, what are they?

What do I want to do with the rest of my life? Do I want to remain single, or do I want to find love again?

How do I find someone new? How do I attract a quality partner? On and on . . .

I started a journal and began writing what I was thinking so later I could go back and see if it still fit. I searched the internet for information about a lot of subjects, including grieving, living a single lifestyle, dating after fifty, relationships, men and women and why they have so much trouble understanding each other, understanding men and why they behave the way they do, why women behave the way they do, self-improvement, the meaning of words like *attraction* and *love*, sex after fifty, etc.

I had no idea there were so many "relationship" experts and dating coaches, and I was surprised to learn that much of what I had been taught (or learned) in the past regarding men was not correct according to today's "experts." I began to think that men were just too complicated or too fragile, and perhaps I should just be happy with my new single lifestyle and forget about a new relationship. I thought, *"Why would I want to have a relationship with a man if I had to be so careful about what I said or did not say to them?"* The whole idea of a relationship seemed to be too much work, and I decided to put the idea of a relationship on the shelf for a while.

As I completed the exercises I included in this book, however, I rediscovered myself and slowly began to make some progress toward fitting the pieces of the puzzle of my life back together. I was able to remember why I had done the things I had done and why I had made the choices I had made. Thinking about the things I liked and the things I didn't, I rediscovered why I felt about them the way I did. I learned that I wanted to make quality decisions and that knowing my values was helpful in fulfilling that goal.

Let's talk about you. Are you a positive person or a negative one? Do you like yourself, or do you wish you were different? Suppose I asked you to make two lists. In one list, write all the things you like about yourself, and in the other, write down the things you dislike about yourself. Which list do you think would be longer?

Studies show that the second list is almost always longer than the first. Why? Because it is generally easier to think negative thoughts than to think positive ones. Why is that, I wonder? Remember the session about doing the opposite of what you feel like doing? Feelings are most often negative and make us feel bad. Changing those feelings to positive ones will cause us to feel better.

Is there something about yourself you wish was smaller, or bigger? Do you know that most of the time, other people don't even notice the one thing about us that we think is a "sore thumb"? I will give you an example. There is a spot on my chin that is all I see when I look into a mirror. It is monstrous, yet when I mentioned it to my daughter, she said she hadn't noticed it until I pointed it out.

It takes only one negative comment to start an avalanche sometimes. Someone will make a negative statement, then another has to agree with him. Pretty soon others offer their negative stories, and the conversation spirals down, etc. This usually continues until someone says something positive. Usually everyone in the group is feeling depressed and they can't remember how they got there. The only way we can change a downward cycle is to *stop*! We must consciously make a decision to change how we think about things. Thinking before you speak is good advice. Think about how the other people are going to feel depending on what you say.

To build up our self-image and regain our self-confidence, we must stop thinking negative thoughts. Instead we must start thinking about our positives and our strengths. If you are a person who dislikes the way you look, then consider this scripture from Genesis chapter 1: "In the beginning, God created heaven and earth . . . God created man in his own image . . . male and female created he them . . . God saw everything that he had made, and, behold, it was very good . . ."[1]

God created you in his own image! Not only that, but it says that he was pleased with his work. Yes, he thought everything was very good. That includes you and me. Do you see beauty in the plants, the rivers and oceans, the birds and beasts? God did! People are included in the beautiful things that God made. He created man in his own image, and then he created a woman from that man! God looked at everything he made and found them beautiful. He was proud of everything he had made, including people. He created *you*, and *you* are beautiful! Remember that!

Here is a piece I found in the newspaper, written by someone who remains anonymous. and I think it is good advice.

"Self-love" (anonymous)—
"If you are not being treated with the love and
respect you deserve, check your "price tag."
Perhaps you've marked yourself down. It's "you" that
determines your worth by what you accept.
Get off the "clearance rack" and get behind the
glass case where "valuables" are kept.
Bottom line, "value" yourself more.

The following several exercises are designed to help you find your positives, your beauty, your strengths, and your values. They will help you to prepare for your future. What is it that you want the rest of your life to be? No matter what you decide—stay single or find a partner— the first step is to learn to love yourself. I am not talking about being selfish here. The fact is that you cannot love others unless you love yourself. You may be thinking, *What is there to love?* It is time to find out the answer to that question now. Your objective now is to become the best person you can be so that you can love yourself.

Where are you right now? Are there any changes you would like to make in order to improve your self-image, discover your self-worth, and gain the much-needed self-confidence that you are going to need to survive this rainy season of your life?

Exercise 1: Stand in front of a floor-length mirror and ask yourself the following questions and write the answers in your journal.

Right now, am I the best person I can be?
What changes in my appearance do I need to make to look the best I can look?

What changes in my attitude do I need to make in order to become the best person I can be?

Loving yourself is important because it is the foundation for gaining a better self-image and for becoming more self-confident so that you can achieve the desires of your heart.

Exercise 2: On a page in your journal, list all the qualities you like about yourself. Be specific. Make three columns and list the qualities under the appropriate category heading. Remember, the goal is to fill the whole page. Here is an example:

Physical:	Personality.	Accomplishments:
my eyes	happy person, positive, active,	I am a college graduate."

Exercise 3: When you have finished filling the whole page with the attributes you like about yourselves, start writing sentences using each of the words and phrases you wrote in exercise 2 telling why you like that attribute. Here are some examples:

Physical—I like my eyes because they are a vivid shade of blue, which changes to match the color of blue I happen to be wearing at the moment.

My Personality—I like my warm personality because I enjoy being with people and making new friends.

My Accomplishments—I like that I am ambitious and hardworking. I enjoy setting goals and working toward achieving them. These traits helped me to become the first person in my family to earn a college degree.

Be sure to leave lots of room under each category so you can fill the entire page with the attributes you like and the reason why you like them. Do not use qualifiers, such as "I wish I were twenty pounds lighter." Qualifiers are not allowed. Remember, we are learning to concentrate on your positives!

Exercise 4: Next, take all your good qualities and write a short third-person paragraph telling about yourself. Write it as if you were talking about someone else. Use this example: "I like [your name]. I really do like _____ because she (or he) _____."[2]

Make a copy of the above exercises and post your answers so that can read then aloud every day. These will become your affirmations. (Note: Feel free to add to the list as you grow).

CHAPTER SEVEN

Values and Boundaries

Please finish exercises 1–4 before starting exercise 5. These questions are designed to help you discover your core values, and they may require some deep soul-searching to answer. At least they did for me! In fact, I almost stopped answering them because I thought I could not answer them; they were so difficult. However, I am glad that I stuck with the task and completed the exercise because the answers helped me to rediscover myself and find out what was important to me. This helped me to discover my values, and also my deal breakers.

"Why is it important to know my values?" you may ask. The answer is because they give us purpose and direction so we can make decisions more easily and to set our boundaries. Think of your values as a compass by which you can compare the activities that come your way. For example, someone asks you to do "xyz," and you ask yourself, "Does this match my values?" or "Is this something I believe in and want in my life?" If the answer is yes, then you can do it, and if the answer is no, then you do not do it. Values make decision-making much easier, and they can help us keep from making a bad one.

Exercise 5. Carefully consider each question below and write your answer in your journal. That way you will have a record for the future, and as you review what you have written, it will be easier to discover your values. Please respond to each question in the order in which it appears below.

1. Suppose someone is giving a speech about you twenty years from now. What would you want them to say?
2. What would you most like to do if you had the time and money?
3. How would you define a true leader? Make a list of leadership qualities.
4. What would you do if you knew that you could not fail?
5. Name two or three people who are an inspiration to you and tell why you think they inspire you.
6. What would make your personal life more fulfilling?
7. What are the biggest changes you need to make in your personal life? If you decide to remain single? If you decide to find a new partner?
8. What activities do you most prefer to do?
9. What are your strengths?
10. What are your weaknesses?
11. Do you finish all the projects that you start? If the answer is no, why don't you?
12. What have you accomplished that gives you the most satisfaction? The least satisfaction?
13. Name three of your greatest accomplishments or achievements so far.
14. What is the hardest thing in your life you've ever had to? Had to overcome? Had to accept?
15. What two steps could you immediately take to make a big difference in your current situation?
16. Do you believe in God? Explain how and why.
17. Do you believe in yourself? Explain how and why.
18. What kinds of things drive you crazy?
19. If you had a magic wand, what would you change in your personal life?[1]

When you are finished, read over your answers and look for patterns to see if you can identify your core beliefs and values. Next, look for the deeper core value within each response. Get to know your strengths and your weaknesses, your likes, dislikes, wants, and needs.

CHAPTER EIGHT

What Do I Want?

Do you remember when you graduated high school and started thinking seriously about your future? Was it easy for you to decide what you wanted to be when you grew up? or was it difficult? Now is the time to think about that question again. Your life was probably already on track as a couple, but now you are single and things are different. Change is always difficult and it is even more so when thrust upon you suddenly or violently as in the death of a loved one.

Sometimes during this grief journey of the past two years, I have wondered if there is a light at the end of this tunnel. I am beginning to think it I will never feel better again. How about You? I am so tired of feeling sad all the time. I miss my husband and I am sure I will never get over my loss, but I think it is time to move on. I am getting used to doing things alone. I am still occasionally overcome with sadness, and my eyes swell with tears, but I give myself a few minutes to remember him and then I wipe the away the tears and continue what I was doing. I think it is good to remember, but it is also good to get back to my well-being.

How are you doing? Are you learning to accept what has happened to you? Have you begun to make some changes in the way you think about things? Remember, that the goal is to think positive thoughts and to be the best person possible. What changes have you begun? Are you making any headway toward looking or feeling better about yourself? Are you getting out of the house and talking to people? Are you learning something new?

Exercise 6: The following questions are helpful in making a decision about the kind of lifestyle you want to live. Do you want a single lifestyle? Do you want to find love and romance again? Ask yourself this set of questions as you think about your future.

- How do I feel about meeting someone new? Am I positive or negative? or in the middle?
- Does my heart feel ready for a new partner?
- Why might I want a new partner?
- Why might I want to stay single?
- Am I happier being alone or with others?
- What are my major priorities right now?
- Do I have time to get involved with another person?
- Have I allowed myself to grieve? to heal?
- Do I want to date just one person, or do I want to play the field?
- Are my emotions under control?

Relationships are not always easy. In fact, they can cause us to feel like we are rding on a roller coaster. One minute we are up, and the next we are down. To be "in love" and to be loved is euphoric; it makes us feel good, and that gives us a real "high"! We feel so happy, we seem to walk on air. But when something goes wrong, doubt creeps in, and that euphoric feeling comes crashing down. We wonder what we did or said that caused the loved one to pull away. Negative thoughts creep in, and we are stirred up. Sometimes it is best to just patiently wait it out, and sometimes, a conversation is needed. To start that conversation, simply ask, "Are you OK?"

It is important to stay positive, but sometimes our friends will try to bring us down. We must learn some strategies for dealing with our negative friends. Sometimes we fill face rejections and we need to learn some strategies for dealing with them. They are a part of life. Perhaps this list will help.

- Remember it isn't about you; it is about them.
- I am sure you've heard these before—"When life gives you lemons, make lemonade;"
- Say "Next...!"
- Take your time when making decisions about your future. There is no hurry. Remember who won the race between the "Hare and the Tortoise"? The slow, but steady, tortoise surprised everyone.
- Be patient and focus on the positives.
- Enjoy each day as it comes and make each day a good one.
- Don't attempt to force a relationship.
- God's timing is not always your timing, but he will have something good in mind for you.
- Live your present in a natural and pleasant way.
- Keep yourself busy, active, and prepared.
- Remember God is working for you in the background and His timeline is not the same as yours.
- Think about the advantages of a single lifestyle and write them in your journal. 1) you can do what you want to do, 2) go where you want to go when you want to go.
- Being single means freedom. There is no one telling you what to do. You are the master of your fate.
- Stop using the word *alone* as in "I am alone," and use the word *single* instead. This is a positive shift because the word *alone* carries with it a feeling of negativity, whereas the word *single* indicates positive feelings. For example, singles have a good time, they live a swinging lifestyle.

If you are thinking about searching for a new life partner, be sure to consider these questions below as we will be discussing them in future chapters.

- What attributes do I want my new partner to have?
- Where does one go to meet available singles?
- How does one start a conversation with someone new?
- How does one go about attracting someone he or she might like to get to know?
- What does one have to do to be more attractive?
- What is attractive?
- What is attraction?
- How can I become more attractive?
- What is love?
- What if my adult children object?

CHAPTER NINE

What is Attraction?

According to www.vocabulary.com, the root word of attraction is attract and its definition is (1) "to exert a force that draws something in, like the way a magnet attracts a paper clip." Another meaning is something that (2) is "pleasing or appealing to the senses, like good-looking, sexually alluring."[1]

When a man is attracted to a woman, he is drawn to her like a magnet. He wants to spend time with her and get to know more about her. She may or may not be drawn to him, but if she is, then we say that the two of them are attracted to each other, or they like each other.

What causes one person to be attracted to another? Kevin P. Ryan claims "there are five scientifically proven ways in which a man is attracted to a woman . . ."[2] (www.businessinsider.com, 2009.) These ways include the following:

1. *Laughter.* Most people are attracted to others who are happy and fun to be around. A woman who is receptive to a man's sense of humor and laughs at whatever he thinks is funny plays into his need to be respected and connects with him on a deep level.
2. *Smile.* A smile is a pleasant gift we give someone. Let's face it. People look better with a smile on their face, and to smile at someone makes us feel better. A smile is usually returned, and

that make us feel even better. There are forty-three muscles in our face, and when we smile, our body releases neuropeptides called dopamine, serotonin, and a whole mixture of feel-good chemicals.

3. *Honesty.* An honest person exudes confidence. Both honesty and confidence increase one's attractiveness.

4. *Wearing red.* Studies show that sexual attraction and desirability are increased whenever a woman wears the color red.

5. *Mirroring a man's body language.* The article suggests that whenever a man is telling a story, if he leans in toward the listener, then the listener should also lean in toward the speaker. If the leader sits back and puts his hand on his face, the listener should do the same. If the leader shows excitement, then the listener should also. Mirroring the language helps to make a connection and builds rapport.[3]

Numbers 1 and 2 above are obvious to me and perhaps to you, because it is definitely more fun to be around a happy person than a sad one. Happy people tend to smile more than sad people. Studies have proven that laughter heals the body by releasing the "feel good" hormones into our systems and the more we are able to laugh and smile, the healthier we will be.

In regards to number 4, I never liked the color red when I was in my teens for two reasons, (1) I thought it didn't look good on me, and (2) it was my little sister's favorite color and she wore it a lot. Strangers would stop and comment to me, "Isn't she cute?" She was cute and perhaps I was jealous, but I left the color red for her. However, I remember I finally bought a red dress in my late fifties, and now that I think about it, I always received a compliment when I wore that dress. I guess I should have taken notes from my sister many years ago. After reading this article a few weeks ago, I decided to wear it to see what would happen. It did seem that more people smiled at me than usual, and a few of them smiled and said, "Hello!" Wow! Maybe I will start wearing red more often.

Number (5) "mirroring a man's body language?" I think that is ridiculous! People, in general, want others' undivided attention when they are talking. Many of us are not really good listeners and maybe this is a good idea. However, what is wrong with looking the speaker in the eyes and showing an appropriate emotion? Or asking an appropriate question which shows interest? Mirroring their body language seems to be an exaggeration.

What makes someone an attractive person? Does he/she have to be extraordinarily handsome or beautiful to be considered attractive? The answer is no. To be attractive, however, a person must show neatness and cleanliness by wearing clothes that are clean and neatly pressed (or at least are not wrinkled). The clothes should fit well and look pleasing on the person, and hair should be well-managed. Most women are more attractive with some makeup. Gaudy, overdone makeup, however, is not attractive.

Other attributes considered to be attractive are: confidence, enthusiasm, having high energy, looking and acting happy and being positive-minded.

CHAPTER TEN

What is Love?

When two people are attracted to each other, they spend more and more time together and when they begin to have strong feelings for each other, the next step might be love. What exactly does the word *love* mean? According to www.dictionary.com, *love* is defined as "*a profoundly tender, passionate affection for another person; a feeling of warm personal attachment or deep affection, as for a parent, child, or friend; sexual passion or desire.*" Other definitions include "*being in love with someone,*" and "*having a gentle feeling of fondness or liking for another person.*"[1]

The English language is confusing because the word *love* means different things depending on who or what follows the word. For example, *love* means something different in each of these sentences: "I love Joan," "I love ice cream," "I love my kids," and "I love to travel."

The ancient Greeks were right to choose a different word for each type. The Ancient Greeks' Six Words for Love are explained by Roman Krznaric,[2] as follows:

- 1. Eros or sexual passion and desire. It was named after the Greek god of love and fertility.
- 2. Philia or deep friendship, comrade with no sexual attraction.
- 3. Ludus or playful affection between casual lovers or children.

- 4. Agape or love that one extends to all people.
- 5. Pragma or long-standing love, the mature, realistic love that develops between two people over time.
- 6. Philautia or love of self which the Greeks considered the healthiest form of love because it encompasses the idea that if one likes himself/herself and feels secure, then he/she has plenty of love to give to others. The idea that one cannot love someone else unless he/she loves himself or herself comes from this form of love.
- Aristotle recognized an unhealthy form of Philautia which is called Narcissism. A narcissist is a person who is self-obsessed and focused on personal fame and fortune.[2] I think self-compassion might explain this love better.

There are two other types which Krznaric did not mention. (1) Mania or obsessive love in which there is an imbalance between Eros and Ludus and means neediness. (2) Another is Storge which is the love parents have for their children.

I think you will agree that having a word for each type of love could help communication. Below is an example of a conversation about *love* I recently had with a man I have been dating.

He said, "I love you, but I am not in love with you."

I paused a moment as I considered what he had said, and then I asked, "What is the difference?"

He immediately responded, "Don't you know?"

"I guess I am not sure. Please tell me what you mean."

He began to explain, "I love you like I love my daughters and my friends, but I am not *in love with* you. I was in love with my wife. I knew when I first met her that she was the one I wanted to be with all the time for the rest of my life. I like you a lot, but I am not *in love with* you."

"So, are you saying that you fell *in love at first sight* with your wife?" I asked.

"Yes," he replied.

I couldn't resist a quip. "Well, you were only eighteen then. What did you know?"

We laughed, and then I continued, "I don't believe in *love at first sight. Love* takes time. We can *like* at first sight, and we can *lust* at first sight, but I don't think we can *love* at first sight."

He was silent, and I continued, "The phrase in *love* is almost always followed by the preposition *with. With* is a function word that indicates another participant."[3] It automatically involves another person, so both people must share the same feeling. *Being in love* with someone means that love goes both ways."[4]

He countered, "But there is another kind of love in which one person loves someone who does not love them back."

I agreed, "Yes, that is called *unrequited* love. One person can love another without being loved back. However, I believe that one person cannot be in love with someone who is not also in love with them."

He said he would have to think about that.

A few days later, I asked three of my women friends to explain the difference between loving someone and being *in love with* someone. The results are as follows:

1. The first one (who was alone in the car with me) explained, "*Being in love with* someone is only *infatuation.* Infatuation doesn't last. Love, on the other hand, does last. It grows and develops over time. It is deeper and lasts longer."

2. I made the mistake of asking the other two women at the same time. One started to say something similar to that above, then joined with the second, as she explained, "*Love* is what you feel for your children, but you are *in love with* the person you marry."

When I got home, I went back to the dictionary to find the meaning of the phrase *in love* and found the phrase was used only as part of the definition of the word *love.* I did, however, find the following synonyms for the phrase: *infatuated, intoxicated, mesmerized, overpowered, seduced, sent, smitten, sold on, stuck on, tantalized, thrilled, titillated, transfixed, transported, under a spell."*

Most of those words and phrases also are followed by a pronoun, usually *by* or *with*.

Erich Fromm, a famous psychoanalyst, made this interesting observation, which is quoted by Krznaric in his article: "We expend too much energy on falling in love and need to learn more how to stand in love. Pragma is precisely about standing in love, [which means] making an effort to give love rather than just receive it."

I decided to look up the meaning of the following words which came up in most or all of my conversations about in which *love* was discussed:

Infatuation is a feeling of foolish or obsessively strong love for . . . someone or something.

Lust is an intense sexual desire or appetite for someone; a yearning, craving, desire, or passion for.

Affection is a feeling of liking and caring for someone or something, tender attachment, fondness.

Passion is sexual desire.[9]

The use of the words *lust, infatuation* and *passion* evoke in a woman a negative reaction, whereas the words *love* and *affection* evoke a positive one. For example, if I tell a woman that I am looking for a *spark, her body* tenses as she shakes her finger at me (as if I am naughty) to correct me, saying that I am looking for the wrong thing. "A *spark* is just *lust* and lust doesn't last You should be looking for "love! Love takes time to develop." However, if I tell her that I meant *chemistry* or a *connection*, then her body relaxes and she says wistfully, "Ah, yes. Chemistry." I have had this same conversation many times and the reaction has always been the same.

I have also discovered a difference between men and women when talking about sex. A man tends to say, "having sex", while a woman tends to say "making love." Interesting.

In the definitions above, the words *passion* and *sexual desire* were used with both the words *love* and *lust*. That was surprising to me although it shouldn't be. I have come to the conclusion that *lust* is the magnet or attraction that draws two people together, and if it holds them together long enough, then *love* develops. Love is the bond (glue) that keeps them together over time.

I have often thought that the reason the divorce rate is so high is that people got married thinking they were in love when in reality they were *in lust*. For most couples passion lessens over time and unless they make a conscious effort to *fan the flame*, the eyes of one or both of them begin to roam seeking to find someone else who can bring that passion back. Again, if love has not had time to mature, then divorce can happen unless there is a strong sense of commitment to each other.

I am reminded here of the Bible verse which defines love.[1]

> Love is patient, love is kind. It does not envy, it does not boast, it is not proud. It does not dishonor others, it is not self-seeking, it is not easily angered, it keeps no record of wrongs. Love does not delight in evil but rejoices with the truth. Love always protects, always trusts, always hopes, always perseveres.[10] (1 Corinthians 13:4–7 NIV).

Recently, I had one of the men I dated ask me, "What has love got to do with it [sex]?" I responded without a pause, "Everything!"

Below I have included a list of signs that help us to know whether or not we really love someone. It was created by Theresa E. DiDonato, PhD, a social psychologist and associate professor at Loyola University in Maryland. You are in love in the following cases:

- You are addicted to that person and want to be with him/her all the time.
- You really want your friends or family to like this person.
- You celebrate this person's triumphs (even when you yourself fail).
- You definitely like this person, and this person likes you.
- You really miss this person when you're apart.

- Your sense of self has grown through knowing this person.
- You get jealous but not suspicious.[11]

DiDonato continued to say, that if love is passion, security, and emotional comfort, then commitment is the necessary (moral and cultural) decision. . . to be with that person.[12]

I think love is a commitment, and the glue that keeps a couple together. I was sad to discover that *commitment* is now a bad word, among senior men especially. They do not want to make a commitment. I hope that *love* does not also become a bad word.

Many women wonder how they can be sure that the man they love, really loves them back. Sabrina Alex offered this list.

- The way he looks at you.
- He wants to give to you.
- He treats you like a priority.
- He wants to immerse himself in your life.
- He really sees you. He doesn't just love you; he loves things about you.
- Your happiness is as important to him as it is his own.
- He misses you when you're apart.
- He keeps you in the loop.
- He's there for you even when it's inconvenient.
- He doesn't give up.
- You don't worry how he feels; you just know.[13]

Bella Popa is responsible for the following list which enables a man to know that a woman truly loves him.

- She supports your passions.
- She wants to get to know your friends.
- She's pleasant with your family.
- She compliments you all the time.
- She's passionate about you.
- She's patient with you.

- She's eager to discuss the future with you.
- She openly communicates with you.
- Your arguments are had with the intention of fixing the issues.
- She doesn't try to change you.
- She does little things for you.
- Her friends have taken an interest in you.
- She's not judgmental toward you at all.
- She compromises with you.
- You just feel it.[14]

CHAPTER ELEVEN

Men and Women Are Wired Differently

Wired differently? That's a new idea! Everyone knows men and women are different and that those differences are quite obvious. But I have often thought it would be helpful if a man came with a manual and/ or a dictionary to help women understand him and how he thinks. Let me explain, I was married to the same man for fifty years, but I have to admit there were times when I just didn't understand. In fact, once in a while he would say, " You just don't understand." He was right. I didn't. There seems to be a universal inability to understand the opposite sex. That is the reason behind my suggestion that men should come with a manual and perhaps women should come with one too.

About a year after I became a widow and decided I would like to have a companion, I discovered the audio course, "Understanding Men," by Carlos Cavallo, www.thedatingadviceguru.com. As I was listening to this insightful e-Book, and wishing I had known some of these things about men, I decided to invite some of my women friends to listen to the course with me and discuss what I was learning. I invited four women, two were divorcees and two were widows like me and we met once a week for several weeks. One widow dropped out and those of us who stayed learned a lot of practical advice we could use in our dealings with men. It was interesting that the two divorcees and the two widows held opposing views about some of Cavallo's ideas.

In the introduction, Cavallo states that the material is based on data he gathered from his work with thousands of men and women over the last ten years. Because of his statement in the beginning that "most women have it all wrong about men,"[1] some women automatically assume he is placing the blame for any problems with men on women. I do not agree. I have a son and a daughter and they are very different in the way they do things and the ways in which they think so I think Cavallo's ideas on pretty much on the mark. Below, I have printed Cavallo's comments first, then follow with my own comments.

1. "Suppose your man has a good reason for what he does. Suppose he is genetically programmed to act a certain way and cannot change his behavior. Could this [knowledge] make a difference in your reactions to his behavior? And would this [knowledge about men] make a difference in your relationship?"[2]

    I believe the answer to the above questions is, "Yes, definitely!" Most of the arguments between my husband and me began with a misunderstanding and my feelings would get hurt because he was not doing or saying what I thought he should be doing or saying. I think had I understood this first concept, I would have been more patient with him and attempted to find out exactly what he meant. For example, I could have allowed clarification simply by repeating what I thought he said and asking him, "Is that what you meant?" Instead, I would get angry and then explode.

2. "Men are not wired to think about two or more things at the same time." They are simply not able to multitask like a woman can. [3]

    I never realized that men cannot multitask. I guess I never thought about it, I do it all the time. Cavallo suggests that understanding this one concept would allow a woman to plan ahead so she can avoid interrupting him when his mind is occupied with something else. I now know that it takes time and effort for a man to switch gears (or subjects) and I need to be more patient with him. I remember my husband telling me that I "flitted" from one thing to another too quickly and he couldn't keep up with me.

A few weeks ago, my pastor's sermon dealt with some differences between a man and a woman. He used an analogy from *Men Are Like Waffles and Women Are Like Spaghetti*, a book written by Bill and Pam Farrel in 2001 which explained that men's brains are compartmentalized. Each of their thoughts and activities are in separate sections. Picture a dinner plate which has the meat, potato and vegetables separated and compare this plate with one containing spaghetti noodles and meat sauce all mixed together. The latter represents a woman's brain which allows her to think about several things at once.[4]

Women have this innate ability to multitask, and that is why they can monitor the kids' activities, fix dinner, chat on the phone all at the same time. I must add here that I have discussed this subject with some senior men who disagree. They think they can multi-task. However, my forty-year-old son agrees wholeheartedly with Cavallo.

3. If a woman understands this concept, she can schedule her want to talk times at a time that is convenient for him. Examples of bad times for a woman to attempt a conversation with a man include the following: (1) when he is watching the news or a sports event, (2) whenever he is reading, and (3) whenever he has just gotten home."[5]

    Cavallo also advises that a man needs to be able to chill for a short time when he first gets home so that his mind and body can make the adjustment from his work environment to his home environment.[5] Cavallo also tells us that this adjustment cannot be made while he is driving home because his mind is occupied with the traffic instead of resting. My son agrees with this and calls it "vegging." If the man is allowed this alone time, then his attitude and well-being will be greatly improved for the rest of the evening. Once he has made the necessary adjustment to being home, then and only then, is he able to start communicating and playing with the children.

4. "Men are direct, saying exactly what they mean."[6]

I do not agree with this statement because I know men sometimes say the direct opposite of what they really mean just to test a woman's reaction. Cavallo even contradicts this statement later when he advises a woman to look at what a man does rather than what he says.

In later years, I learned that my husband's definition for some of the words he used was different than mine. I wish I had known this earlier. This is why I think men should come with a manual that includes their own dictionary. Perhaps this would help solve the problem of the sexes being able to communicate with each other.

I agree that women tend to hint at what they want instead of being direct. This may happen because they are afraid of hurting his feelings or that he will be angry with them, and they want to avoid an argument.

5. "A man is his opinion, and disrespecting his opinion is disrespecting him!"[7]

I have come to realize that this statement could very well be true as I have recently experienced a man walking away from me very soon after I had expressed an opinion that was different from his.

6. "Once a man has made up his mind about something, it is almost impossible for him to change it."[8]

I have noticed several profiles on the dating websites that state, "I am a Liberal, and if you are not, please do not contact me." Talk about a closed mind.

7. "Men have a stronger sense of self than women do."[9]

I agree that women are wishy-washy. My husband once told me I was wishy-washy. I thought I was offering him a chance to choose the restaurant (for example) that night. I think women are overly concerned about what others think about them and, therefore, are afraid of saying the wrong thing. Both men and women are sometimes insecure or have poor self-images.

8. "Men fall in love more quickly than women."[10]

This statement was a surprise. I think most women would be surprised too. However, when we stop to remember that men are visual creatures who tend to pay more attention to the way a woman looks rather than her other attributes, it is easy to see that he can fall quickly for a beautiful-looking woman. A woman, on the other hand, while she may be attracted to a man's physical appearance, tends to study his personality to see how he acts so she can determine if he will meet her needs.

9. "Men want to be appreciated."

Cavallo says that most men do not receive much praise during their lifetime. When they are little boys, they tend to be considered troublemakers, and whenever they get hurt, they are told to "suck it up", "be a man", and "don't cry." While little girls are told how "cute they are" or "You did a good job, honey," etc. A woman needs to tell her man that she appreciates him and the things he does for her. He needs to know that she has his back. However, she must be truthful in her praise because he knows when he is lacking in this department, and her appreciation will be labeled "false."

I definitely agree with Cavallo on the above statement, but I want to add that women also need to hear that they are appreciated. Too many women will work harder and harder to please her man in order to earn his love, but it has the opposite effect. Men tend to think she works hard to please herself.

The other day, one of my friends was telling me about her deceased husband, and she mentioned that he often would tell her to leave whatever she was doing and come sit down with him. That sparked a memory of my own husband, who would say something similar. I would always be hurrying up to finish whatever I was working on and say, "If I don't get this done, it will never get done," and continue what I was doing. Once I joined him on the deck without him requesting it, and he said, surprised, "You mean you are actually going to sit down with me for a few minutes?"

At the time, I didn't know why he was so surprised, but now I know it was an important time for us to be alone, just to chat and spend some alone time together, which is what he wanted. I had unknowingly given priority to all the other unimportant things instead of giving my time to my beloved. What was wrong with me? Nothing. I was just being a woman! Sad!

10. A man wants three things: (a) to be helpful, (b) to solve problems [fix things], and (c) to feel useful.[12]

My response to each of these three things is as follows:

a.   My husband told me he wanted to be more helpful around the house. But because I always complained that "he didn't do a good job" or "what he did wasn't good enough," I destroyed his desire to help me. I ended up having to do everything myself because no one else could do it "right" or according to my standards. By being overly critical, I ended up hurting myself, and I learned too late that it is better to accept whatever a man offers to do and not to judge him or his results if I want him to continue to give his help.

b.   My husband was definitely a fixer. He enjoyed fixing things around the house. He did this willingly (most of the time) for me, and I did always thank him for it and praise him for doing a good job. However, it is important to know that at times, a person just wants to vent and is not asking for advice on how to "fix" or solve the problem. Everyone must learn to recognize when the other person is just venting and when they are asking for help or a solution. Sometimes, the only thing needed is a good listener.

   c. As my husband grew older and became physically unable to fix things around the house or do the jobs he once had done, such as yard work, driving the car, etc., he felt useless, becoming embarrassed and degraded.

To reiterate, a man will work harder to please the woman he loves if she is vocal with her praise, admiration, and appreciation, but he loses motivation when he is subject to sharp criticism and lack of respect. It is important to remember that a man may be criticized a lot at work and should not have to be criticized at home.

11. "Men are born hunters. They love the chase, and they love to win."[13]

The experts all agree that men are meant to be the chasers and women are emphatically advised to allow the man to do the chasing. In fact, over and over again, the message I get is that to keep a man's interest, a woman must continually challenge him to earn her love and respect. It is a complete waste of time and energy for a woman to work hard to please a man, thinking it will make him love her more, when in reality that is what drives him away. To keep her man, a woman must find new ways to make her man work for her love.

12. In short, Cavallo admits, "Men want a sex object, and women want a success object."[14]

What can I say? It is in a man's DNA to make babies and assure the future of our species.

13. What do women want in a man? According to Cavallo, A woman wants a man who is educated, has ambition and wealth, is respected, has status, is tall and strong, dominant, assertive, has strong facial features and a good sense of humor [which shows intelligence, novelty, and flexibility], and willing to make a commitment. [15]

    When I discussed this statement with my women friends, they disagreed and gave me a different list. They want a man who is kind, caring, honest, understanding, thoughtful, clean, handy, old-fashioned, a gentleman, and a good dresser.

14. "A man will never be able to love a woman like she wants him to love her." [16] This is because a man loves differently than a woman does. What he wants is respect, and that is love to him. [17]

    A man shows that he loves a woman by providing for her, protecting her, and doing things for her. A woman needs to learn to recognize that these are the signs that he loves her. She needs to notice what he does and understand that he is doing it for her. He is showing her he loves her by helping her. A woman needs to allow a man to help her whenever he offers.

    Can you let (allow) a man to help you? Do you step aside when he offers to do something for you and let him do it? It will improve your relationship when you do this.

15. "A man wants to make a woman happy, and if he thinks he cannot make her happy, then he will leave her alone." [18]

    I was surprised to hear Carlos say this, but I am now convinced that this is definitely true.

Steve Harvey made the following observations in his book, *Act Like a Lady, Think Like a Man*, which I found easy to read and very enjoyable. Harvey says:

> A woman who genuinely wants to be in a committed relationship . . . must be able to understand what drives a

man, what motivates him, and how he loves. If she does not understand these things, then she will be vulnerable to his deception and to the games that he plays. . .The game a man plays is to do whatever it takes to get the woman he approaches to sleep with him.[19]

Again, what can I say? I believe them to be true.

CHAPTER TWELVE

For Women Only:
Avoiding a Big Mistake

This chapter is for women only. Men, please skip this chapter and go straight to exercise 8. In that exercise (8), the assignment is to make a list of the qualities you are looking for in a woman. Women will also do exercise 8 and make a list of the qualities they are looking for in a man before going on to chapter 13.

The advice in this chapter is extremely important because women make this serious mistake all the time. What is this big mistake? Cavallo claims that a woman who says, "I love you," before her man says it causes him to run in the opposite direction.[1]

He does not explain the reason why this is true, but I think it is because he has not made his decision as to whether he loves her or not. Remember that he likes to be the chaser. Once he hears her say those words, he knows he has won! Then he thinks it is time to move on and start another chase.

Another thing that happens is that he begins to feel obligated, which causes him to feel trapped. He does not like that feeling and, therefore, begins to pull away.

Cavallo advises a woman to subtly make her man aware of the ways in which he benefits because he is with her. In other words, she needs to let him know, in a subtle way, "what's in it" for him to stay.

Exercise 7: Make a list of the ways in which he is benefited because of you. Then you will want to be prepared for the right moment to casually slip one of them into a conversation. Do not preach!

I admit that when I was first started this exercise, there were four things that immediately came to mind. They were sex, cooking, laundry, and cleaning. However, my friend John and I worked together, and we came up with the following list.

I am your "eye candy." You like to show me off.
I am a very good companion.
You enjoy doing things with me.
I am fun to be with.
I make your life fun.
I like to do things with you.
I like to go out with you.
We like to do spontaneous things, on the spur of the moment.
I look attractive, and you enjoy watching me when I don't know it.
You enjoy watching me in action.
I listen when you talk.
You enjoy our conversations.
I am good company.
You enjoy traveling with me.
I show you that I appreciate you.
I tell you that I admire you.
I encourage you, and you feel like a better person when you are with me.
You like my physical contact.
You like me to touch you.
I like you to touch me.
You like to cuddle with me.
You like holding hands with me in public.
You feel better when we are together.
You like the way I make you feel.
I understand you.
I "get" you.

I make you feel safe.

I allow you freedom to be with your friends occasionally.

I allow you to maintain your independence.

I help you with chores.

I allow you to "help" me.

You like it when I allow you to do things for me and vice versa.

I prepare good meals for you.

I keep your house neat.

I help you with your laundry.

I help you with our finances.

I help you to have a fun social life.

I help with your decision-making.

I accept you and your differences as a man.

I understand where your thoughts come from.

I know what drives your desires and influences your emotions.

I connect with you on your level.

I know how to keep you attracted to me, and I use it wisely.

I work to build the kind of connection with you that we both want.

PART THREE

Dancing

CHAPTER THIRTEEN

Dating is Different Today

"Dating today is different than it was fifty years ago," my daughter had said when I first brought up the subject of dating again. She is correct in many ways. Society has changed, and so have we. Our goals, attitudes, wants, and needs are all different today than they were fifty years ago. Back then, we were excited about falling in love and living happily ever after. The goal for most of us was to get married, have children, and live in a beautiful house with all the fixings. Today we have been there, done that. Our children are now grown and, hopefully, pursuing dreams of their own, hopefully, with families of their own.

Life does not treat everyone equally. Some seniors have led relatively happy and carefree lives, while others have not. All have lived through some good times as well as bad. Many may have issues that are hard to deal with. Either way, change is difficult.

Today, many seniors just want to have fun and/or companionship. Hopefully, they are financially secure and in relatively good health so they can pursue those goals without being a burden to their children. Most are able to enjoy their grandchildren. Many are babysitting to help out the young families. Some are overburdened with the care of the younger families and unable to enjoy what retirement offers. Some seniors like the freedom of a single lifestyle, and others would like to find love and romance again. Some seniors want to play the field, some want a monogamous relationship, some want no commitments, some want to get married again, and some just want sex.

Society has changed so much that things once kept private are now public knowledge. Sex is openly discussed and blatantly advertised. It is in the movies, music, magazines, books, the internet, and computers. It is even considered an acceptable topic of conversation among senior men and women. In fact, I have been frequently asked the question, "Are you still interested in sex?" within the first ten minutes of a conversation. Other questions I have been asked are "Can you still do it?" and "Do you do oral?" One man told me he had no trouble getting it up, but he didn't know if he could get it in.

Remember when we were twenty and some of us had the rule, "I don't kiss on the first date"? Today the kiss is expected, and many men expect to have sex on the first date. With some, it is a given on the second date.

Even though our bodies are not as flexible as they used to be, and we may not be able to do some of the things we once did, we still want to do them. Our need to love and to be loved doesn't disappear just because we are older. Those who have been married have been accustomed to having frequent sex, so when a spouse dies, they ask, "What are we supposed to do now?" Adult children mistakenly think that their elderly parents are no longer interested in sex. They are wrong.

Other topics of conversation between men and women who are dating include the medications each are taking and for what reason, prostate cancer, condoms, sex toys, oral sex, and other some subjects I never heard of before.

A major challenge of today is dealing with our own adult children who have very definite opinions about how we are supposed to act. Their opinions are sometimes the opposite of our own. They may think they want to protect us from getting hurt, and most prefer to think that we do not have sexual needs and desires. The reality is they are jealous and concerned about our money.

More important, seniors need to know that careless sexual activity has dreadful results. Age does not protect us from getting sexually transmitted diseases (STDs) and infections (STIs), and we need to know how to protect ourselves from them. They are very serious problems.

According to WebMD, in 2012, the rate of sexually transmitted diseases (STDs) more than doubled among middle-aged adults and the elderly over the last decade.[1] Without the worry of getting pregnant, older adults seem to forget that there are worse things that can happen to us. One man asked me for a date, then decided he needed to tell me he had genital warts and asked if I have anything against that condition. I told him that I didn't know anything about them. He told me to do a Google search and I did. I decided not to go there.

Here is some more information I found online at www.webmd.com:

Sexually transmitted diseases (STDs and STIs) used to be called venereal diseases (VD), and are among the most common contagious diseases in the world. More than sixty-five million Americans have an incurable STD, and each year, twenty million new cases are reported. Half of these infections are among people ages fifteen to twenty-four, although this is changing to include people over fifty. All infections have long-term consequences.

The germs that cause STDs hide in semen, blood, vaginal secretions, and sometimes saliva. They are most often spread by sexual intercourse, including vaginal, anal, or oral sex, and include just about every kind of infection.[2]

Please learn all you can about this subject and be careful!

CHAPTER FOURTEEN

Our Adult Children Object

Handling our adult children's objection has become a huge problem for many seniors. Some seniors yield to their children's desire instead of pursuing their own goals and dreams. Others blatantly tell their kids to mind their own business. Some of the issues are as follows:

(1) The kids prefer to think their parents don't have sexual needs and desires.

(2) The kids are just plain lazy, refusing to get jobs, and continue to "sponge" off their parents.

(3) Sometimes grandparents choose to raise their grandchildren because their own kids are ill, on drugs, or have died.

(4) Many young people are accustomed to a lifestyle they cannot afford so they take advantage of their parents and refuse to leave the "nest".

I have found in many cases, adult children who continue to live at home do not even help with the household chores. If the elder parent agrees to allow their adult children to live with them, then they need to set some rules and if the young people want to live there, then they must follow the rules. The young people must be told there is no "free" ride and it is up to the older parents to enforce their rules and practice tough love, even to the point of finding help to force the kids to become responsible.

An article on the eHarmony dating website, "Handling Our Adult Children's Objections," gives a lot of information about this subject. The author states that senior adults "have every right to meet new people, start new relationships, and build a new life." and that seniors should never allow anyone to discourage them from dating and/or getting married again, if that is what they want to and are able to do.[1]

The article also states that the two reasons our adult children object to us finding a new partner are time and money! It all comes down to the fact that they are jealous because our new relationship is taking our time and money away from them.[2]

Seniors and their children need to sit down and have a serious conversation covering these issues: (1) that we love them and will continue to make time for them, but that we intend to have fun with other seniors; (2) we need to answer all their questions about our finances, including information about wills or trusts, because they need to know our financial affairs are in order; (3) that they have their own lives to live and so do we.

It is suggested that we try to find out the real reason for their objections. Here are some questions that we need to ask:

- What would you like to achieve with your negative feelings?
- What effect is my new relationship going to have on our relationship?
- Do you think your attitude and behavior are going to affect my relationship with the person I love?
- What would you like to see happen?

We need to tell the kids that we are upset by their behavior and are torn between wanting to please them and wanting to move on with our lives. We need to be firm with them about the fact that we need to move on. Ask them to give your partner a chance, and if they refuse, try to keep the two relationships separate.[3]

Change takes time, and hopefully, when they see you enjoying life again, they will accept your decision. If nothing else works, just ask them, "Don't you want your mom [or dad] to be happy?"

Remember it is natural for our children to want to protect us. They don't want us to get hurt emotionally or financially, but we are adults, and now is the time to put ourselves first! If we are lonely and want to find a new love, then we should go for it. We raised our family and took care of our responsibilities. Now we deserve to enjoy the fruits of our labors. If we don't do it now, we never will. If we want to travel, then now is the time to do it. If we want to date, now is the time to date. Who knows what our future holds? Statistics show that health really begins to go downhill after eighty which makes travel impossible. Many people put off their retirement until it is too late and they are unable to do what they want to. Please do not let this happen to you.

If you haven't done this already, make your bucket list. This is a list of things you would like to do when you retire. If you can't think of anything to put on it, then ask yourself, "When you are on your deathbed and someone asks what is the one thing you wish you had done but didn't, what would your answer be?" Will it be, "I wish I had done more babysitting?" What would it be? Think about it, then write it down and do it.

I think our children ought to be happy that we are not a burden to them. They probably haven't thought about that, but they may be called upon to take care of you sooner rather than later. Enjoy the good years you have left before it is too late.

Genesis 2:24 states, "Therefore, shall a man leave his father and his mother, and shall cleave unto his wife."[4] Perhaps at this time of our lives, it should read "a man (or woman) shall leave his/her adult children and cleave unto his/her significant other.

If our children are old enough to enjoy sex, then they are old enough to suffer its consequences. I realize that in some cases, such as illness or death, grandparents may have to take on the job of raising their grandchildren, and they deserve praise for their efforts. But I am disgusted that so many young adults do not step up and accept their responsibilities and rights of being an adult. I think they should be ashamed of themselves if they are taking advantage of their elderly parents at a time just prior to the role reversal, the kids taking care of their parents.

I have an eighty-year-old male friend who continues to allow his two grandchildren to live with him as well as his three great-grandchildren. He babysits the three little ones while their mother works, and as I understand it, he provides the food on the table, gas in the car, and pays their cellphone bills. Doesn't this sound like elder abuse? He is stressed out, with headaches all the time, and still babysits these three little ones. One child is an infant, one is three years old, and one is seven years old. Neither grandparents nor great-grandparents were meant to be full-time babysitters. Once in awhile and for an hour or two, that is enough! More than that should not even be considered as far as I am concerned.

Sometimes, the adult children are physically abusive when they don't get their own way. Outside help may become necessary to force the freeloaders out of the nest. I know it is difficult to have to do this, but that is why it is called tough love. If your rights are being abused, then you need to get help. There are agencies available whose job it is to see that our rights are not being taken from us. Call your local police for more information.

A friend recently complained that his twenty-six-year-old grandson refuses to get a job and then told me a story about a ticket the young man had gotten while driving grandpa's car and grandpa was out of town. My friend went to the police station and paid for the ticket. I responded that the young man has no need to get a job as long as his grandpa continues to pay for all of his expenses. I think that as soon as a child turns eighteen, he/she is an adult and as such needs to become fiscally responsible. It is a proven fact that people do not value the things they are given. It is through their own hard work that they begin to learn the value of money and then and only then do they begin to respect money and to make better decisions about how they spend it.

I once asked my friend, Jim, who had been divorced thirty-five years, if he had any advice I could put into this book. He enthusiastically arose to my challenge because he had experienced this problem several times in the past. He had witnessed several women who were too generous with their retirement savings and had ended up giving it all away in bits and pieces to their children and grandchildren. The result of their generosity was that they became penniless and desperate to find a husband who would take care of them. These women really annoyed Jim and he wanted me to advise women in my book to become better money managers and to safeguard their savings by refusing all requests for money. Remind everyone to do this in order to survive their own later years. Otherwise, they will become "needy" and this kind of person is extremely unattractive. Most people do not want to be around a "needy" person and if a new husband discovers his new wife was destitute, he feels "used."

While I am on this bandwagon, I know that many parents think it is their responsibility to pay for the college education of their kids. If they can afford it, then that is their decision. However, most people have enough problems just taking care of themselves. I used to feel guilty because I couldn't afford the college tuition for my kids until one day I heard Suze Orman, a popular financial adviser, tell her television audience that a parent's responsibility was to provide the necessities for their children until they turned eighteen, and that whatever was left over after paying those necessities, was to be saved to pay for their own needs in retirement! To be fiscally responsible, it is most important for parents to save for their own futures. College is not a right nor a necessity and, therefore, it is the responsibility of the person who wants to go to figure out how he/she is going to pay for it. It is not their parents' responsibility! Seniors' earnings begin to dwindle as they get older even as their expenses continue to rise. Because of this, seniors need to set aside money to take care of themselves until they die. I heeded this advice with my own children and did not feel guilty about it.

Since people value the things they earn more than what is given to them, if students work to pay for their own college education, then perhaps they would spend more time studying than partying.

Suze Orman is right. As I mentioned earlier, in retirement our income will be fixed while expenses continue to rise. Who is going to take care of the seniors whose money runs out? As my friend Jim suggested, please begin now to say *no* to all requests for money. You are going need that money for your own survival.

Here is an example which happened to my mother. In 2012 she had a car accident which caused her to spend the next five years of her life in an assisted-living facility. The cost of this was $5,225/month. That came to $62,700/year and $313,500 for five years. How much money do you have in your retirement account? Considering that prices will continue to rise, will you have enough money to last as long as you do? This is a huge concern for most people, whether they will have enough money to live on until they die. Ask yourself, will your children be able to take care of you if your money runs out? For the greater majority of seniors, I fear that the answer is most likely *no*!

CHAPTER FIFTEEN

About Online Dating

Now is a good time to take a look at your journal entries and see what you decided about your future? Do you prefer living as a single adult? or do you want a new adventure? Would you like to find a new companion or a new partner?

While living with my daughter, I decided I wanted to find a new friend, someone with whom to go shopping or out to lunch. However, after a while, I decided I wanted more. An immediate challenge for me was that I had few opportunities to meet people because I lived out in the country and the towns nearby were quite small. So, I decided to check out the internet dating websites and see what I could find. The following statistics were given on www.datingsitereviews.com:

- 58 percent of singles meet dates through friends.
- 37 percent meet dates in bars, coffee shops, and other public areas.
- 27 percent meet in the workplace and/or at events.
- 49 million people in the United States have tried online dating.
- 46 percent of dating app users met their current partner online.
- 46 percent of people have a positive attitude toward dating services.
- 19 percent of adult singles in the USA say they are registered on a dating service.[1]

I became one of 49 million people in the USA who have tried online dating, and now (in 2020), I am one of the 46 percent who met their partners online. It took me awhile.

Some of the men I chatted with back then told me that they had been on a dating website for ten years or more. My immediate reaction was, *I wonder what is wrong with him.* Before I found what I was looking for a year ago, I began to wonder the same thing about myself. In fact, I had a guy asked me, "What is wrong with you?" (I wonder how long it took him to find someone?)

At that time, I asked my friend John, "Am I being too picky?"

He replied, "No, you are being selective, and that is what you need to be!" That made me feel a little better. He is such a nice man!

As you read my story, I am sure you will be wondering why I put myself through *this*! Perhaps you also may think, you would never do that! Several women have told me this and I am OK with it. To each her own.

I chose a different path. That is for sure. Since I had moved to a new area and I was retired I did not know where to go to meet men. I went to two different senior centers, but saw no one I wanted. I don't drink or go to bars. I find myself saying hello to those in the checkout line at Meijer and Walmart, but that has not brought forth a coffee date yet. Church is a good place to meet people, they say. But I have never received an invitation for coffee there either. I finally discovered the singles dances, but that yielded dates with only two different men. That left me with online dating websites.

Advantages of Online Dating

- You don't have to get dressed up and go out to meet a really nice person.
- You can set up a profile on the computer to be your people magnet to match you with men who have similar interests while you work or sleep or just hang out!
- If you are shy, the privacy of the internet offers you a chance to engage in conversations with people you would not approach in real life. It also gives you the chance to practice your flirting skills.

- A computer database provides a wide selection of candidates with similar interests.
- It actually works!

Disadvantages of Online Dating

- Many men on dating websites are only looking for sex and not a real relationship.
- There are many scammers who set up fake profiles to attract vulnerable women and men with the idea of stealing their money.
- It is difficult to tell if the person with whom you are chatting is telling the truth.
- Men and women send outdated and/or inappropriate photos—nude, sexy, etc.
- Some crazy guys fall in love almost immediately (note: scammer!).
- Scheduled meeting dates are sometimes canceled or are no-shows.
- Unanswered messages cause a person to feel rejected.
- Some men online just want to talk with someone and have no intention of having a long-term relationship.

Here are seven types of men you will find on dating websites, who will be a waste of time, so choose not to go there.

1. Men who only want a pen pal. They are lonely and just want someone with whom to chat and keep them company.
2. Attention seekers who desire validation and want their egos stroked.
3. Emotionally unavailable men.
4. Players.

5. Angry Men.
6. Mr. Hook-Up just wants sex in person or on the phone.
7. Those who want to borrow money (scammers), which is never returned.

In spite of these disadvantages, I encourage anyone who wants to find love again to try online dating as long as he or she has some computer skills and follow the rules I am going to set out for you in this and subsequent chapters. Here are a few absolutely necessary points to keep in mind:

- Always treat it like a game and have fun with it. If you cannot do this, then don't do it.
- Maintain a good sense of humor, a good self-image, and exhibit self-confidence.
- Maintain a healthy mindset.
- Think of it as a fun activity.
- Keep your messages fun and your conversations light.
- If it is not fun for you, then don't do it at all!
- Some men do it because it is more interesting than television.

I learned the following information from Michael Fiori's e-course entitled "*Online allure* and I created the chart below, "Five Kinds of Men on Online Dating Websites."[2]

Five Types of Men Online Dating Site[s3]			
Male Type:	**Goal 1**	**Goal 2**	**Goal 3**
1. **The sex shopper**	Sex	Sex	Sex
2. **The commitment addict**: To be avoided because they are often emotional physical abusers and are extremely jealous.	Ego	Gratification	Control Sex
3. **Scammers**: To be avoided because they are liars and cheats.	Money	Money	Money
4. **Nice guys/really good guys**: A majority of men on the web fit into this category. Shy guys are often great guys but they are lacking in self-confidence. They have incredible approach anxiety and are scared of women in one way or another. They are often frustrated and even a little angry, and they use online dating because it allows them to talk to girls without the fear of talking to them in person	Sex	A Girlfriend	Companionship
5. **The Alpha Male:** Has plenty of confidence; takes up space in the room; has an effect on women and usually dates multiple women at once because he can; he is charming because he has lots of practice. He has a job or owns a business or feels powerful in his everyday life; is very attractive; and is extremely frustrating to women. In short, he is a *player*.	Sex	Ego	Vague About the Future

CHAPTER SIXTEEN

Getting Started Online

If you have decided to try online dating, I suggest you research several dating websites to see which ones will work best for your needs. You can do this by Googling the words *dating websites* to read about the different websites and what they have to offer. Some sites allow you to look at photos and profiles for free, but it is necessary to buy a subscription if you want full use of the website. The six-month subscription is usually best value for the money. I also suggest that you purchase a subscription for two different websites so that you are able to maximize your exposure, you do not want to put all your eggs in one basket.

Once you have made those decisions, you will begin answering questions for your profile. This is the web page that tells about you and what you are looking for in a partner. Needless to say, it is important to be truthful about your information because you want your date to recognize you when you meet them. Otherwise, they may not like what they see and walk out on you on your first date. This will certainly not help your self-confidence. A good relationship cannot be based on a lie!

Your profile will include your age, height, education level, profession, interests, and whether you are a "woman looking for a man" or a "man looking for a woman." Be careful which of those options you check because your profile will end up on the wrong side if you make a mistake. I have seen a few women's profiles on my pages, which obviously were mistakes, or they are not looking for me. Be sure to save your answers often.

Think of an attention-getting headline and a pen name and tell just enough about yourself to pique the interest of a quality candidate. You want to motivate someone to send you a message of interest. Don't tell too much! You want to have something to talk about when you get together in person.

Tell something good about your work, what you do for fun, something you are passionate about, and a little about your personality. Show your confidence and be sure your words are light and fun! *Save your work.*

Avoid using words that make you appear "needy," such as "princess looking for my prince" or "I didn't want to do this, but my sister [or brother] signed me up." Absolutely do *not* write anything suggestive or sexy! Remember, you are a quality person who wants to attract a quality person, so be sure your writing reflects this message. Simply tell who you are and what you want.

You will need to upload some attractive photos of yourself. One of them needs to show your full and smiling face. Another might show you actively involved in something you like to do. Do not include photos of you with other people unless it is very obvious which one is you, and no photos of animals unless you are also visible in the photo. Nude and other suggestive photos are not allowed. Remember that you are a quality person, and a quality person does not do such a thing. It is in your best interest to look good!

Once you have finished answering all the questions, uploaded your photos, and saved your work, your profile is "live" on the internet, and all candidates with whom you are a match will be able to see it. You will be the "new kid on the block," and you may receive several messages at once. Some people want to chat with only one person at a time and some want to shop around. I prefer the latter, but it is time-consuming and sometimes confusing to carry on several conversations at the same time. I have even sent a message to the wrong person. That was embarrassing! I solved this problem by printing their profile page and writing information as I learned it. I also used 3 x 5 cards to help me keep track of several at the same time.

Remember, your goal is to get to know enough about a person so you can decide if you want to meet them or not. Then you want to schedule that first short meeting as soon as possible. The reason for this is to avoid wasting a lot of time chatting and then find out when you meet in person that there is no connection. Schedule this first meeting within the first two weeks if you can. If this is not possible, then move on. Don't waste any more time with that person! I have found that in small towns this rule has to be flexible. But, I do try to get a meeting right away.

It is very important to remember that you are very vulnerable when meeting a stranger and that is what you are doing. You must always remember to protect yourself. It doesn't matter how much time you have spent chatting with this person, you do not know them and you need to be safe. This is my checklist before each "date."

- Schedule meetings in a safe, public place during daylight where there will be lots of people, like a restaurant.
- If you are a woman do not give a man your last name, home address, telephone number, or any other personal information until after the first meeting.
- However, it is important for a woman get your date's full name. phone number, make and color of his car and license plate number before your first meeting.
- Leave a written message of the above information in an obvious place in your house so that your family can easily find it in case you disappear.
- Always drive yourself to the meeting place and, should you decide to go somewhere else, drive yourself there alone!
- Do not get into your date's car and do not let him/her get into yours.
- Women, don't allow your date to walk you to your car after the first meeting. If necessary, ask an employee of the restaurant to walk you to your car.

- Always think about keeping yourself safe.
- Men, if you go to a stranger's home, remember that you do not know who is on the other side of that door and that it could be a man with a gun. Be sure you are safe too.

As you read the profiles and your messages, remember your boundaries, and when someone crosses them, block them or stop responding to them. The following are some rules to note and remember:

1. Block anyone who goes sexy in the first message, appears to be a scammer, obviously has not read your profile, does not answer your questions, or sends you a message that is insulting or hateful.
2. Warning signs on a guy's profile include pictures of himself with other women, shirtless pictures with his guitar, badly lit pictures, and the use of poor grammar and misspelled words.
3. If you ask questions that are not answered, you are not having a conversation, so stop writing and forget that person! Seventy-four percent of singles identify good conversation as the single best indicator of great chemistry on a date.
4. If the message sounds strange, do not respond. It is probably a scam. Block it!
5. If you get no response to your message, it is not a big deal. It could just be bad timing. It is not about you! Wait at least two weeks before writing the same person again. If there is no reply after the second message, forget them!
6. It is OK to take the initiative if you are a woman.
7. Just because one guy/girl isn't interested in you does not mean you aren't interesting! Remember, this is a game! Say, "Next!" and move on.
8. If you get a bad response, don't force the issue. Cut the cord and move on. Stay positive and relaxed. Ignore the rejections.

According to Zoosk.com, most of its members are looking for love and romance. They reported that if the following phrases are included on your profile—*old-fashioned* and *hopeless romantic*—you will generate more responses than if you do not include them.[4] Remember:

YOU DESERVE THE VERY BEST! DO NOT SETTLE FOR ANYTHING LESS!

CHAPTER SEVENTEEN

Communicating Online

It is always advised to utilize the dating website's chatting and messaging platforms, which are safe and secure. Do not move to personal email or telephone numbers until you get to know more about the other person. Always think safety. Be careful that you don't give out too much personal information too soon. Once your full name is known, anyone can easily find out the rest on the internet.

One red flag of a scammer is that you are asked almost immediately for your personal email or cellphone number. Several reasons are usually given, such as so you can get acquainted faster or the other person is busy and unable to come to the dating website very often. Do not fall for it! Once you give out your private email address or cellphone number, the other person's profile almost always disappears quickly. This means they are not a paid subscriber, and they are phishing. Beware of them.

For those who are unfamiliar with the different means of communication online, I have printed the following definitions from the Wikipedia Online Dictionary.

> Text messaging is the act of composing and sending electronic messages between two or more users of mobile devices, desktops, laptops, or other type of compatible computers. Text messages may be sent over a cellular network. . . or via an Internet Service (SMS). . . but

has grown to include. . . digital images, videos, and sound content, as well as ideograms known as emojis or small images. Text messaging is a quick and easy way to communicate with friends and colleagues when the two people are not required to be present at the same time. It was first used in 1992.

An E-mail is a text document which is sent to your Internet Service Provider server when you press the 'send' button. There it sits for a little while, from a few microseconds to an hour or so, waiting for the mail server to process outgoing email. This document is transmitted as a single file, including attachments, to another server, the recipient's Internet Service Provider's incoming mail server. . . The message then resides on the incoming server until it is downloaded by the recipient.

Instant text messaging is a series of data packets, sent as the "send" key is activated, then are routed by whichever way is available, to another computer. However, many ISP text servers are operated in a batch processing fashion, so the text messages may sit in the outgoing server for a second or two."

Online Chat is a conversation between two or more people at computer keyboards. . . and are sent without delay, to each computer that is logged into the chat session.

Which method is fastest? "Email is fast, text messaging is faster, and online chat is the fastest."

Communication begins on a dating website when one person sends a message of interest to another. The recipient receives an alert text message on his or her own cellphone or computer and then must log in to his or her account online in order to read the message and respond accordingly. I suggest checking your messages frequently because the best conversations take place when both people are online at the same time. Otherwise, it may take days or weeks for a conversation to take place.

Most of the time, it is rude to carry on long text conversations in front of a third person. It is best to wait until one is alone to read the message or to quickly read it to see if it is an emergency, but then put away the cell phone until later. In some cases, it is OK to send a short reply telling the sender that you cannot "talk" right now. If a longer reply is needed, then it is better to excuse yourself and move to another room to reply. This is the same action you would take if you receive an important phone call.

It is a good idea to observe how your friends handle their calls and text messages in front of you, and respond accordingly. Some people are offended if you carry on a long conversation with a third person in front of them.

Be sure to read your message before sending it because the automatic spellchecker can substitute words you did not mean to write, and you may be embarrassed when you do read your message.

Again, I caution you to be careful about the information you give to a stranger on the internet. You do not know if you are chatting with an honest person or not. The person might be a criminal. He/she may really be currently in prison, a nursing home, or anywhere.

I did not know that one of my contacts was a man who was living in a nursing home. I soon found out that he was looking for someone to take him out of the nursing home and take care of him. We do not know what we do not know. The internet protects each person's privacy.

According to an article found at www.datingsitesreviews.com, "on average there are 25,000 scammers online at any time, talking with a potential victim. . ."[1] The article also reports that "500,000 of the 3.5 million profiles on dating websites it scans every month are fraudulent." Always think safety first and do not give out too much personal information. Absolutely do not give out any of your financial information and do not believe everything you read on the internet!

PART FOUR

Be Careful

CHAPTER EIGHTEEN

Danger Lurks

Unfortunately, there are always people who take advantage of a good thing and ruin it for everybody else. This has definitely happened to online dating, and I am now sharing important information about romance/dating scams as they are called. This type of scam has become a multimillion-dollar illegal business and is growing by leaps and bounds. A recent report from Federal Trade Commission states that online dating scams were the "costliest scams reported to the FTC in 2019." $201 million in losses were reported, which is an increase of six times since 2015 when it was only $33 million.[1] Thousands of people have lost millions of dollars from their retirement savings, which they will never get back.

I found that some people do not know they were scammed. Several men and women have told me that they were asked for money and gave it to them. They said it was just a donation to someone in need. They were all surprised when I informed them that they had been scammed. Anytime someone on the internet asks you for money, stop communicating with them and contact the FTC or the website on which you met them.

One thing I find amazing about this is that the same people who give the money in this way would most likely hang up on a telemarketer. How is this any different? That is a good question! Yet many men wire money to a voice and photo of a pretty young woman and never realize they have been scammed! Women wire money to handsome men who look successful.

Scammers are criminals! They are liars and cheats who steal photos and profiles of attractive men and women (who are also victims by the way) to post on dating sites as their own in order to attract lonely, unsuspecting, and vulnerable single women and men. They then spend time chatting with their victims, pretending a romance, earning their trust, and then steal their money. Scammers send professionally written messages to a number of possible victims and wait for a reply (sounds like a fisherman throwing out his line?). When they receive a reply, they respond with well-scripted template messages. They consider a very good prospect to be those who respond to their first message. Over a few hours and days, the predator "falls in love" with the victim, and a bond of trust is established. Soon there is some type of emergency, and they need to "borrow" some money. Of course, this is urgent, and the money is needed immediately. The victim might first be asked to send a $50 iTunes card or Steam card. This is just a test to see if the victim will comply. Once they succeed in getting the small amount, their requests will be for larger and larger amounts as the relationship continues.

So many people are falling for these romance scammers despite many public warnings from the authorities and the media that is has become almost an epidemic. The scammer almost always asks for a loan, which will be paid back as soon as possible. However, the money is never returned, and in most cases, the victim and the scammer never even meet each other.

Consequently, the scammers are extremely good at what they do, and many victims are giving away their life savings to these criminals. Please become aware of this problem and be very diligent in your dealings with people you meet on the internet. Do not allow yourself to become one of their victims! Asking for money is the absolute proof that you are talking with a scammer. Please see chapter 21 for more red flags.

Do you hang up on telemarketers? Do the same with these scammers. Especially if someone asks you to send them money, just hang up! Have you heard about the "Suckers Lists"? Perhaps not, but maybe your name is already on one, and you do not know it. If you have sent money or an iTunes card to anyone you have met online, then you have been scammed, and you are a victim. Your name is now on a "Suckers List." How does that make you feel?

Perhaps you have fallen in love with the photo of a handsome, successful-looking American businessman who tells you that he has just won a contract for work or a project in a foreign country and must leave tomorrow. Did he tell you how beautiful you are? Did he tell you that you are the one he wants and that he is already in love with you? Did he describe the beautiful future the two of you are going to have together? Rest assured that he will soon have some type of emergency and ask you to wire him money ASAP. Or perhaps you have already wired him the money. If so, then you are a "victim," and your name is on the "Suckers List." How does that make you feel?

There it is! Once you have wired, sent, or given money to a scammer, your name is automatically added to a "Suckers List." These lists are sold or passed along to other scammers, just like a telemarketer's list. In a few weeks, you can be assured another scammer will contact you, and you need to block them as soon as you see a red flag. To avoid being put on this kind of list, you must be careful and refuse all requests for money.

I indignantly told my daughter I would not fall for a scammer and that I would not send money to one. But I did. I felt sorry for this man with whom I was chatting for a week, and I ended up sending him some money. Not what he asked for, but some. When I discovered that I had been scammed, I was angry and wanted revenge. The more I thought about what had happened to me, the angrier I became, and after telling my daughter what had happened, I went to the Michigan State Police and reported it. Of course, I already knew that they would not be able to catch the person responsible for this crime, but I thought it would help the authorities to catch them, so I reported the incident.

When my anger subsided, I wanted to warn other people of this huge problem and enable them to just say no! I wanted to tell them to hang up whenever someone asks them for money. In fact, it became my passion, and I decided to write that book I had always thought about writing. Please do not allow yourself to be taken advantage of in this way! I thought perhaps if I told my story, others will heed the warning and protect themselves by keeping their financial information private. Do not believe a stranger who asks to borrow money from you. It is not a loan! You will never get it back! If it is a stranger on the internet, you most likely will never meet the person who says he loves you so much. He has been lying to you. He could even be richer than you. He is involved in a multimillion-dollar business and making about $200,000 a year.

It is my hope that others will read my story and join my crusade to get the message out so that this illegal business will cease. People must stop giving away their money in this manner.

Victims of this scam lose more than their money. They also lose their dignity and self-respect. They are embarrassed and humiliated. Some victims have also lost their lives. Being a victim of a scammer negatively affects the relationship between themselves and their families and friends! Trust is eroded, and a reference to the incident will sneak into conversations at times, reminding the victim of his/her mistake.

Please know that you have the right to refuse any and all requests for money from strangers, friends, and even your own children and grandchildren. You must become a diligent manager of your money because you are going to need your money. You will need your money if you become ill. Please do not fall for a scoundrel's lies and give away your livelihood.

In chapter 13, I have already discussed the fact that, in retirement, you will be living on a fixed income, and your expenses will continue to rise. You must become diligent with your money. It is time for you to be selfish and think of yourself. Do not make criminals wealthy at your expense! Do not allow your children to squander that which you earned through hard work and sacrifice.

First and foremost, a request for money is an immediate red flag of a scammer, and you must not only say no but you must also stop talking with them! This is true whether the person making the request is someone you have only been talking to on the internet or someone you meet on the street. It is not in your best interest to give your money away! Just say no! Seniors are susceptible to all kinds of scammers, and we need to be aware that this happens. We must learn to say no and stand our ground. I was having a conversation in McDonald's the other day with an acquaintance who confided that a woman he dated had asked him to loan her $2,500 for something she said she needed. Because he felt sorry for her, he loaned her the money. A few weeks later, her son told him she had spent the money on drugs. How do you think he felt? He felt awful! He was scammed! He was a victim! Do not let this happen to you!

There have been more than a million victims of romance scams in the US, and although the media and law enforcement agencies have been trying to educate the public about this crime, people are not getting the message. Giving away money to scammers has become an epidemic. Some people think they are too smart to be duped in this way, but no one really knows what he/she will do in a given situation until it happens. According to a Wymoo International Investigators report, "romance scammers are experienced criminals . . . who understand the game they play better than anyone. They are especially dangerous . . . Every word in the conversation is planned (and recorded) so there (are) no inconsistencies . . . Everything is calculated so that no one . . . can uncover the fraud."[2]

These scammers are polished professionals who utilize professionally written scripts designed to win the affection and trust of their victims. They are extremely patient and good at what they do, and they use techniques like brainwashing to gain the trust of their victims, who are almost hypnotized into doing what is asked of them. Widows and widowers are a major target because of the assumption they have lots of money from recent inheritances. Most scammers think that their victims have a lot of money and can afford to share it with them.

American men are very susceptible to beautiful young women who plead for gifts of money or iTunes cards. American women are attracted to handsome and successful-looking men offering love and romance.

A former scammer testified that he had made $800,000 in a period of four years. He said that he had "taken" it from only a handful of victims.

Do you still feel sorry for those pretty young women because you have money and they do not? Think again because most likely they are wealthier than you are.

Christians are taught to be generous and to help the poor, and these criminals use this trait to their advantage. These "brainwashing" techniques play on the emotions of people, and rational thinking "flies out the window." Only later do the victims "wake up" to discover they will never get their money back. Neither will they ever meet their scammer.

The privacy of the internet makes it very difficult for the authorities to find these criminals. Some of them have been discovered and put into prison. But many people are still being victimized. It seems to me that if people would just stop giving them money, the business would stop being profitable, and therefore, it would stop. I have joined this battle against this terrible epidemic by writing my story and trying to educate my readers. You can help by passing along the information. Perhaps we can stop this outrageous conduct!

Currently, the criminals are winning, and seniors are losing the battle as more and more become victims. We must stand together, develop our backbones, say no to all requests for our money, and mean it. We must not allow them to manipulate us into changing our minds and giving in to their demands. We save ourselves only by ending this travesty! The only reason criminals are winning so far is because we are losing. This losing streak of ours must end!

Please pass on this information to all the people you know and meet, and if you are chatting online right now with someone who sends you beautiful love letters and exhibits other warning signs of a scammer (see chapter 21), stop talking to them immediately. *Block* them and report them to the dating website and to the authorities. If you are the victim of a romance scam, file a complaint with the FBI's Internet Crime Complaint Center immediately.

A request for a loan or iTunes card or cash is evidence of illegal activity. You must refuse those requests and block them immediately, and you must report them. You can report them at www.fbi.gov. Report it to your local police if you are being victimized or have been taken advantage of. Your rights have been abused.

Whatever you do, do *not* send money, and do *not* give them your social security numbers, credit card numbers, or banking information. Also, stay safe by withholding your last name, address, and/or phone number from people you do not know well. Keep the names of your family members private also. You do not know how strangers will use this kind of information you give them.

CHAPTER NINETEEN

Scammers' Victims Speak Out

There are now several websites that list the names of scammers and give other information about them. There are also websites that share the stories of scammers' victims. A Google search will bring up this kind of information. This chapter tells some stories of victims.

Number 1—In July 2019, Dr. Phil McGraw featured a woman whose two daughters sought Dr. Phil's help in convincing their mother that she was being scammed. The woman proved to be so entirely vested in her "romance" that she was absolutely convinced she was married to the actor Tyler Perry, even though she had never met the man in person. Here is how Dr. Phil advertised the show.

> Dr. Phil received an urgent anonymous email claiming the clock is ticking for Karla who's blowing through her retirement fund to please her online love. Karla has lost her job, house and friends, and alienated family members, and has even lost custody of her two younger children. Her two older daughters, Kelly and Kourtney, join together to convince their mother that she must face the truth about her digital marriage dilemma with the help of Dr. Phil. (https://www.drphil.com/shows/

my-mom-is-delusional-she- thinks-shes-married-to-tyler-
perry-and-has-sent-her-catfish-100000/)[1]

Dr. Phil presented Karla with tons of evidence that she
is the victim of a scam, but she is so sure of her romance
she refused to believe him. The only concession she made
was that she would not send any more money to this man.

Number 2—I recently had lunch with my friends, Janet and Judy, and
Janet asked me about my book. Judy did not yet know about it and
wanted to know more. As I told her about it, she immediately piped in,
that she too had been scammed and shared her story with us. When she
told us the amount of money she had lost, Janet was flabbergasted and
burst out with this question, "Why did you do that?" Judy responded,
"Because I was stupid!" I immediately asserted, "You were not stupid.
You were just vulnerable!"

Judy agreed that she was indeed vulnerable, and someone had taken
advantage of her in that state. She continued with her story telling us
that when she realized she had been scammed, she contacted the FBI.
She was told that she was one in several thousands of victims of romance
scammers and that she would probably not get her money back. The
ensuing FBI's investigation resulted in the arrest of her scammer—a
retired priest with Alzheimer's who was living in a nursing home in
Germany. He claimed he had sent the money to his scammer, but that
person was never found.

Judy admitted she felt stupid because this was the second time she
had been scammed. The first time was by someone she knew, and she
thought that she should have learned from that mistake.

I mentioned I had read that many victims say, "It is not just the
loss of the money." A broken heart is more painful than losing some
money, and the loss of self-image and self-respect are painful as well.
The feelings of being stupid, dirty, embarrassed and humiliated are
also difficult to deal with, as well as the loss of a "dream relationship."

Number 3—The daughter of another friend dated a man she had met online for four years before marrying him. Not long after their wedding, she began to notice her savings account was dwindling, and she had not been making any withdrawals. Looking into the matter, she found her husband had been withdrawing money from her account without asking her. When he left for a business trip, she decided to see what she could learn about his activities on his computer. She was horrified when she learned he was still on several dating websites as a single man looking for not a woman but really young women. She also found nude photos of young children in his desk drawer. She called the police and started divorce proceedings. So far, it has not progressed very far because of his claim that she was his accomplice and that she had given him the money. To this day, her family is still trying to help her get free of this man so she can get her life back on track.

Number 4—Women are not the only ones used by scammers. Cal shared his story with me. He had started a conversation with someone in a chat room when there was a "down time" at work. At some point, he began to suspect that he was chatting with a minor and decided to try to find out for sure, so he set up a meeting at a local park so that he could keep on driving if he saw she was a child. When he arrived at the meeting place, a police car was there. He had been set up by the police officer who was looking for pedophiles. Cal was arrested, and at his hearing plead not guilty. Over the next several years, this dragged on and he continued to plead not guilty. Finally, he grew tired of this and decided to plead guilty. This was a very bad idea because he now has a record and is considered a felon. A year or two after this happened a different attorney told him he was wrong to plead guilty because it was the officer who had broken the law by setting Carl up.

Number 5— There was an article on the internet about another male scam victim. His story was that of a woman who convinced him to give a large sum of money to a charity that she was promoting. Once the check was sent, he discovered it had been all a lie.

Number 6—Two men who attend the singles dances were talked into sending money to a pretty woman who claimed to be a doctor and wanted to come to the USA, but did not have the money. Both of these men sent money for airline tickets to these women so they could come to America. After they got the money, they wanted more so that their families could come with them.

Anyone who has been duped by a scammer will admit that the lost money is not as hurtful as the "hit" on one's emotions. It is a humiliating and draining event that is always at the back of the victim's mind. Many feel stupid for having been taken advantage of in this manner. As if that is not enough, many feel guilty for having fallen in love with a criminal, and although they probably have never met in person, most victims grieve the loss of that "love" and their dream of a wonderful future. Anyone who has not experienced being victimized in this manner will never fully understand, and as the victim attempts to explain, the end result is that the victim feels like he/she is the criminal instead of the victim. The scamming incident becomes an ever-present "elephant in the room."

CHAPTER TWENTY

Follow Your Heart, but Lead with Your Head!

Jeremiah 17:9 (NIV) states, "The heart is deceitful above all things and beyond cure. Who can understand it?"[1]

Sometimes our heart can get us into a lot of trouble. Remember the saying, "If something sounds too good to be true, it is!" That is why I say, "Follow your heart, but lead with your head." Our gut feeling tells us a lot, and the wise thing to do is to listen to it. Follow your instincts. This song by Elvis and Frank Sinatra carries a warning for all of us. Perhaps these celebrities would have had better lives if they listened and heeded the words they sang: "Fools rush in, / where angels fear to tread / and so I come to you my love My heart above my head / Though I see the danger there . . . / Fools rush in, / where wise men never go / But wise men never fall in love / So how are they to know / When we met, I felt my life begin / So open up your heart and let this fool rush in."[2]

Perhaps we need to heed the words ourselves and take our time before making a decision. If someone you recently started chatting with on the internet tells you too soon that they have fallen in love with you, remember these:

1. Love takes time to develop and grow.

2. Two people who are attracted to each other must spend a sufficient amount of time together in person doing activities and getting to know each other before rushing into something.
3. Real people do not fall in love from a few written words or only a photograph or a few phone calls.
4. Infatuation may feel wonderful, but it doesn't last.

Love just does not work that way. If you get a text message or email from a stranger telling you they love you, it is an automatic red flag, and you should suspect they are a scammer.

Recently, I found a flyer at my local bank with the following information printed on it, which is good advice whether the person on the other side is a romance scammer or any other type of scammer.

> Scammers are targeting people over sixty years old more frequently and they are using the phone, computer and paper mail. Here are five tips to help you avoid falling for their tricks:
>
> 1. Recognize urgency as a red flag. Phrases like "right now" or "there's no time" can be a clue that something is not quite right. Pause before taking any action.
>
> 2. Never give out personal information to a caller. You can always take the time to hang up, look up an official number and call to verify the situation.
>
> 3. Be wary of clicking links in emails or text messages. These messages may be fakes, designed to steal your login information when you click. Open a web browser and type in the website address yourself if you want to check it out.
>
> 4. Don't repeat passwords across accounts. If you do get tricked into giving your username or password for a

website, fraudsters will use them to try to log into your other accounts.

5. Consult someone you trust. Scammers count on you being too emotional to think clearly. Always reach out to someone you trust – a relative or attorney – for a second opinion. (Anonymous)

All the above are very good suggestions. We must all protect ourselves the best we can, and that includes protecting our money and our emotional health. In fact, if someone you meet through social media tells you that they are in love with you within the first two weeks of communicating and you have not met in person, you need to take that as a red flag and expect that in a few days, they will be asking you to send them money! Recognize that you are the one in charge and just say no to all requests for money (even a loan), then block them! Even if you think you are falling in love with them!

Do not allow anyone to talk you into doing something you will regret doing later! Believe me when I tell you, "You will regret it later because you will never get your money back, nor will you ever meet the person who told you they loved you before asking!"

Make one of your boundaries to block anyone who even hints at needing some money! I have had the person with whom I am chatting slip into our conversation a very slight phrase that when it is analyzed indicated he/she wants me to offer to send them some money. Do not go there! Ignore it, wait and see what happens, or block them now. He or she is a scammer, and you will eventually feel used, humiliated, and ashamed if you send them money or give them access to your financial accounts.

Instead, block their number on your phone or computer and report him/her immediately! Do not tell them what you are going to do. Just do it! A scammer is a very dangerous person. Just *stop* chatting with one and notify the administrators of the website, your local or state police, and www.fbi.gov!

CHAPTER TWENTY-ONE

Red Flags Tell You it is a Scammer

Below is a list of red flags I have accumulated through experience. Every one of them has eventually led to a request for money, which proved that the person with whom I was communicating was a scammer.

Be very careful what you write in a message and say to people you meet on the internet. Scammers can be found in all social media, and although some dating sites are more thorough in attempts to avoid fakes, scammers sneak through all the barriers. I personally have been approached by a scammer on all ten of the dating websites I have used and on all social media, including Facebook and LinkedIn.

Remember, scammers use stolen profiles and photos of attractive men and women to establish fake identities (profiles) on all social media websites in order to attract lonely, vulnerable men and women. Even the real owners of the profiles are also victims of the scammers, because they are unaware of their photos and profiles used in this manner.

How can you tell if a person you are talking with is a scammer? Until someone asks you for money, it is almost impossible to know for sure. But that one request is proof of a scammer. They will deny it and do everything to try to convince you they are real, but do not believe them. They are liars.

I prepared the following list of red flags to help you realize you are communicating with a scammer. You will know immediately whenever you see the following in your messages and emails, especially if there are more than three, except for the asking for money rule. That is automatic proof of a scam. Feel free to print the list and keep it near your computer so it will be handy as you read your profiles and messages. Stop writing immediately and do not waste your time with them.

1. If anyone asks you for your personal email address or phone number right away.
2. If anyone asks you to go to a different place to chat, such as Google Hangouts, WhatsApp, etc.
3. If anyone claims to own his own business, to be an engineer, to be in construction, to be in the military, or to be working offshore or on an oil rig.
4. If anyone claims to be an American but is working in any foreign country.
5. If anyone sends a message but lives too far away from you.
6. If anyone is twenty to fifty years younger than you are, ask yourself, "Is it realistic for a twenty-year-old through forty-year-old to want a partner who is seventy?"
7. If anyone claims to be over sixty-five with a young child. For example, is it realistic for a seventy-year-old man to have a five- to twelve-year-old daughter or son?
8. If anyone sends a photo in which he/she looks younger than the age shown on the profile.
9. If anyone's photo looks like it could have been copied.
10. If anyone has inconsistencies in their profiles.
11. If anyone calls or texts you, and you recognize that the area code that shows on your cell phone does not match the state shown on his/her profile.
12. If anything in the background of their photo does not confirm their location.
13. If anyone cannot be found in an online background search.
14. If anyone's Facebook page shows very few friends or photos.
15. If anyone asks you to stop communicating with others on the dating site right away.

16. If anyone has given you a name that doesn't appear on a Google search.

17. If anyone says they are on Twitter.com or LinkedIn.com, check out the information they gave you to see if what you have been told about him/her is the same on other websites.

18. If anyone schedules a meeting but always cancels.

19. If someone falls in love with you without meeting you, especially during the first few days of communication.

20. If anyone sends you love letters, poems, cute emojis, other images, and links to love songs on YouTube in their texts.

21. If anyone asks you for money or an iTunes card.

22. If anyone sends you email or texts with identical wording you have received from someone else.

23. If anyone who talks with you has a foreign accent.

24. If, when you call their number, they do not answer themselves but give you a recorded message such as, "This text message client is not available."

25. If anyone sounds like they are "in a box."

26. If anyone's voice sounds disguised in any way.

27. If there is background noise, pay attention to it.

28. If there are people talking in the background.

29. If the voice sounds familiar.

30. If anyone asks, "How long you have been on the dating site, and what is your experience?" (May not be a red flag, but if it comes with other red flags, then it is.)

31. If anyone asks, "Do you live alone?"

32. If anyone asks, "What are you doing at that moment?" or "Where you are going now?"

33. If anyone asks, "Have you eaten breakfast [or lunch or dinner]?"

34. If anyone calls you by the wrong name or misspells your name.

35. If anyone's spelling and/or grammar is poor.

36. If anyone does not answer your questions.

37. If anyone tells you he/she makes a six-figure income or more.

38. If anyone tells you he/she owns several large and/or expensive homes.

CHAPTER TWENTY-TWO

Yes, I Am a Victim of Scammers

I believe I have chatted with more scammers than anyone else in the world, because I ignored two of the safety guidelines listed on every dating website advising its members to communicate only on their platforms and to protect yourself by keeping your email address or phone number private until you have chatted for a while and are reasonably sure they are who they say they are.

Because I was curious and thinking I might write a book about the experience with online dating, I wanted to know what would happen. I found out alright and I have wasted so much time because of it! So far, every person I gave my email to when they asked for it right away has been a scammer. The same is true for everyone I have agreed to chat with on Google Hangouts, WhatsApp and or Instagram (except for one).

I was very skeptical throughout my internet dating experience and a little nervous, always trying to be cautious. I created a way to organize the material, and I printed all the profiles of the people with whom I chatted. As I chatted with them, I jotted down notes on the printed profile to help me remember each person. I also printed all email messages and most of the chats, which I copied and pasted into a word document, in case I might need proof of the conversation in the future.

This made it very easy to spot thirty-eight red flags (see Chapter 21) and to create the list.

Except for the one scammer who found my weak spot (an American being detained in China), I resisted the others who asked me for money, and with my list of red flags, I learned to recognize a scammer almost from the beginning of the conversations. I admit that I hoped some of them were for real, but over and over again, it was obvious that "If it sounds too good to be true, it is." In chapter 15, I shared a list of the types of men who are on the internet which helped me to realize what each man's game was, except for the two I share in chapter 23. I still do not understand their game. Scammers use every trick in the book to obtain our personal financial information, and as soon as we say no, they try to make us feel guilty. It is best to block them as soon as you see a red flag. They are not worthy of your time or energy.

This chapter is my chance for revenge. In it you will find the actual emails and messages I received from some of the scammers so that you will learn to easily to know that if you receive something similar, stop communicating with them immediately. Since scammers use other people's names and photos, I have changed the names to protect the innocent. I have enclosed the exact letters as I received them so you will be able to see the misspelled words and incorrect grammar that are red flags that indicate a scammer. If you receive any mail with patterns similar to those in these letters, stop communicating with that writer immediately and report him/her to the website on which you met them.

Number 1—My first scammer was Gerry, who was one of the first people to send me a message. He wrote that he liked my profile and wanted to get to know more about me and asked for my email address "so we could get acquainted faster." He looked and sounded like a really nice person who lived less than an hour away, so I gave it to him. As soon as I hit send with my email address, his profile disappeared from the website. This happened quite often, and I soon learned that it meant he was not a paying subscriber and a scammer.

Gerry never got far enough to ask me for money because I ran a background check on him soon after we began chatting. It was there I discovered he was lying to me. Here are the emails he sent to me:

From: Gerry 1/23/2017 9:08 AM Good Morning Dear, Thanks for the short note. I am so happy i came in contact with you. You are extremely beautiful. I pray you will be the answer to my prayer. I will be willing to start out as friend with you and see where it goes. Let's share some vital information about each other. My Name is Gerry_____. I am 63 years old. I'm presently residing in Columbus, Ohio. I grew up in Belgium. I was born and raised in Brussels. I came down to the states in 1981 to finish my study. I had a Degree in Electrical Engineering. I lost my wife and children 15 years ago due to car accident and now intending to move on with my life with that lovely, honest, faithful woman with so much love to give because I am tired of public settings with dishonest, unfaithful women. The site is very boring as many women are not honest. I am not looking for someone to replace my wife but someone to be herself, know what she wants out of life and someone willing to forget the past and intending to move on for a better future. I am now willing to enjoy life, spend, share time together with that lovely woman that could make things right between us. Being single has been a challenge for me. Having a very strong faith really helps to get one thru the hard times and I thank God for everything. God is a big part of my life. I don't know what I would do without him. He is my rock"

Occupation: I am into (Electrical & Electronics Engineering). I install ELT appliances for Private and public sectors, Houses or Companies. I work for myself. I am a happy man with so much love to give but take honesty as the first step in doing anything and also friends first, we could take it from there and see what develops. I am a good Christian with a sincere, caring, loving heart and hope of a better tomorrow because when there is life our hope should always be high and we should never give up until we finally make our dreams come true and this is the reason why I am taking this chance because we aren't meant to be alone forever. I am a very honest, caring, family oriented, Independent, loving, romantic man with a nice sincere heart of taking care of my own woman, home, respect her and giving her all the love she deserves because I want a woman that I can't live without and same in return.

I am a very optimistic man and love to meet new people with my smile, I am very easygoing, non smoker and Social drinker. I have a great sense of humor, love to laugh, tease jokes, cuddle, swimming, camping. I would love to know more about you. I hope we can become close friends and perhaps even more. All good things, great relationships take time to develop. I will be waiting to hear from you. I attached few pics of myself. Distance isn't an issue when there is an honest communication. I am a good writer and i hope you too. We have to be committed to build a long-term relationship. Attached to this email are my real recent pictures. Please write me back to tell me full details about yourself also and send me some pictures of yourself. Have a wonderful day. ~~~

Here is another one:

Hello Shelby, How was your night? Thanks for your message with the beautiful pictures, and for telling me little about yourself. well, Here is some more about me that I feel that you should know as well. Let me start when my wife and two children, K____ & B__ passed away... My wife was from the Caribbean (Cuba) and unlike most American men, I married for love not tradition.

I remember going out with her for 6 months before we made love. When the exciting day came, she asked me what took me so long, and i said i wanted to be sure that we were both ready for it at the same time and that no one would be hurt. i guess i made an impression because 1 year later we were married.

The day that my family was killed, 01/18/2000. In the morning it started to snow. I had gone to work that day in the morning where i worked in NYC at a very prestigious firm

As the day was progressing the snow was falling harder. The firm decided to give everyone off, so I went to the train station to take the hour 15 minute ride home. Before going home I stopped at the jewelers to pick up T___'s present, an engagement ring that i promised to myself that I would buy her. I came home to find the house empty, with a note stating that Theresa and the children were out doing some last minute shopping and that they would be home soon. I was young, 46 years old because i was born in 'September', dark hair, kind of thin, with a full beard. about 3 in the afternoon, there was a knock on the door… I opened the door to find two policemen standing outside. They asked if I would accompany them to the police station with me. When I asked what was going on, they said that at the moment they could not tell me. I went with them to the police station. Once inside the police station I saw a number of people including some doctors and a psychologist. They sat me in a room, closed the door and the windows, and shut the drapes. I had no idea what was going on or what was about to happen well i was in shock to say the least. they escorted me to the hospital so that I can identify the bodies. I identified T_____ and K__ but B_____'s body was not there. When asked what happened they told me everything that happened. according to an eye witness T____'s car was rammed in the side by another car with so much force that the van split in half, ejecting K____ in her seat from the car. Kimberly had internal injuries but i was able to see her. When she asked me if mommy and B____ were OK, i lied to her and said that they were upstairs and we would see them soon… how can i tell a 9 year old girl that mommy and B___ died… she gave me a hug and a kiss and told me that she loved me. she asked me if i was going to stay in her room a while and i agreed, she winked at me and fell asleep 5 minutes later she died.

The hardest part was trying to tell all the family members that i lost my family. For about 1 year after i was a total mess. I started using drugs (never injecting myself) to forget My job was understanding about my situation, but i started coming to work either stoned or completely out of it. they finally let me go. which at that point was the downfall to my life or so i thought. it took me another 6 months to clean up my act. I was angry, mad, upset, it got to the point that i really did not care anymore. about 6 months after that i decided to work for myself. I still had contact with some of my clients and received numerous references from them. I decided to Relocate to OH to live my life because i had a client who was like a friend there. I decided that i was just going to work, eat, go to sleep and work. that was going to be my routine for the rest of my life. I felt that no one can get hurt. i stopped using drugs, but i still do have an occasional cigarette.

It took me 5 years of constant work 16 hours a day, 7 days a week to get to where i am. At the trial the judge (who happened to be a personal friend of my father) was ready to throw the book at him, when i asked to speak to the court. The drunk drivers wife and children were in the court room at the time and as unconventional as it was, i said to the court as i looked at his two young daughters, and said that his daughters needed him more, then the court needed him in jail. Well due to my testimony, even though, i did mention that he destroyed my family, he received 5 years probation, 3 years suspended license, 5 years alcohol anonymous, and a few other fines. His wife thanked me, i said your welcome and walked out of the court.

Three years ago he came into my office not knowing it was me, and when he saw me, he was ready to walk out. I spoke with him for a while. When he asked me why i did not throw him out of my office, i said to him that he has to live with what he did for the rest of his life, and if he made amends that was great. One day my friend who is an electrician introduced me to his cousin who was from Brazil. a very attractive girl (not as attractive as you). we began seeing each other off and on for about a year. then things started to become a little more serious. but i never was the pushy type, never forcing anyone to do anything they did not want to. perhaps that may have been my downfall.

see i never have nor will i ever force someone to do something, there was a time when we would go to bed, i am sleeping just in my under garments and she was in her thong or g-string. I was reading a magazine and she was reading a book. i rolled over and gave her a hug and kissed her good night, never touching any part of her body but her waist. well i think she was looking for more but i am the type of person that i do not have to make love or have sex every time i am in bed with someone (which is not very often). the next day she was gone and i received a call from my friend a few days later asking me what went wrong. he told me that in her country women are used to being rough handled by "their man" and well that is not me. so i maybe the best thing for me is to be a "Jewish monk" (which by the way there is no such thing as a Jewish monk). As business prospered, so did my lifestyle (remember i did not have a woman, how can i have a lifestyle).

Unfortunately i start getting high blood pressure, went to see the doctor and the doctor told me that i should give up smoking. I gave up smoking and became healthy. Recently, i decided to join a dating site to wipe out my loneliness because we aren't meant to be lonely forever. Destiny led me to you and here we are becoming friends. Hope you can tell me more about your past too. The only surviving family i have now is my brother. Kelly. He is presently in Jail serving Life imprisonment. I hope u can tell me more about yourself too. Have a wonderful day.

Gerry

P.S. My profile was signed up in Bristol, TN the time i went there to execute a project, like i said earlier, I install ELT appliances such as design and testing of electronic circuits that use the properties of components such as resistors, capacitors, inductors, diodes and transistors to achieve a particular functionality.

Note: I had asked in my previous message why his profile said he was from Bristol TN, when he said he was living in Cincinnati, Ohio. He replied he had gone to Tennessee for work and signed up for the website while he was there.

and another

Thu 1/26/2017 9:21 AM Hello Shelby, Thanks for your message and your sympathy. I am truly a magnanimous man. I treat others the way i wanted to be treated. Well, you have pass through some bad moments too. I am sure it makes you a stronger person. Well, i admit we all are human, struggling to get to where we are today. I am Glad you trusted me enough by telling me all this. I feel sober for you. I am a hardworking Man. Well, I can see the reason while u may not want to rush into any relationship. Sincerely, i pray God gives me the opportunity to win your heart and to make you happy for the rest of your life. You deserve happiness. You need the hands that will pamper you and care for you.

Everything that happens in life is Destiny. We need to accept our destiny day by day. We need to forget the past in order to be able to move on to thė future. Change is the only constant thing in this life. And those who look only to the past or present are certain to miss the future. Life can only be understood backwards; but it must be lived forwards. The past is never where you think you left it. The future influences the present just as much as the past. So we have to move on with our life.

Well, I'm God's sent to wipe your tears away. True love is not easy to come about at our age. True love is what everyone talks about but only few has experience it. If we believe in this honest communication, we can be part of the few that will experience it. This is the best way to learn more about each other. I want to be your friend and let's see where it leads to. Every relationship starts with Friendship.

Hon. Love can sometimes be magic. But magic can sometimes… just be an illusion. Love is never lost. If not reciprocated, it will flow back and soften and purify the heart. Baby, clearly, Now i can tell much about you, your past and your hobbies. I promise to care for you if given the chance. You will never have reason to regret being my friend . I will be glad if u can send me more pictures of yourself. Signing off for now. Hope to hear from you soon.

P.S. ...Regarding the my profile on Love and Seek, well, i have turned it down since i have been talking to you and you are the only one i have been talking as i am one woman man, I am not that use to flirting website, so i prefer to stick with one woman than flirting around, meanwhile, my profile on Love and Seek stated as follows' I am a very romantic, caring, fun loving man and I love to dance, laugh, kiss, hug, cuddle and gardening. I am really very young at heart and love to interact with people. I've emerged from the fog I was in after losing my wife. am looking for a honest and reliable woman to be with for the rest of my life. I am Looking for a woman that would grow old with me. A woman that would always be there for me both in time of sorrow and in the time of joy. I am sure there is a woman out there that is looking for the same thing with me, I would be more than happy to welcome such a woman into my life.

I am looking for someone who is spontaneous and non controlling. If you're interested in finding out about me or me finding out about you, please use your own words and I will respond. I'm a tad shy. I love a sense of humor and I don't mind laughing at myself.

I love to dance and love all music, especially the 70's rock, and I love movies and live theater. I take advantage whenever possible of the great talent offered in woman. I'm good, honest, cherishing, caring and loving, passionate and affectionate, honest and reliable, trustworthy and a good man, I have a great sense of humor and god fearing which i believe is the most things in this life and it is so necessary in life."

My comment—When I finished reading the letter about the death of his wife and daughters, I was laughing. I could not believe what I had just read. I told myself this was either the saddest story I had ever heard or he was the greatest liar to have ever lived. There we several red flags: the fact that he had asked me for my email address in his first message, and the poor grammar and misspelled words.

I ran a background check on him, and everything looked OK. I didn't notice anything unusual about it. However, just as I started to delete it, something caught my eye, and I went back to read more carefully. All three names of the women who died in the accident were listed there. But something was different. Their ages were sixty-three and sixty-four and ninety-two. He had written that they all died young many years ago. He had lied to me!

I was still very new at this and considered what I should do. At that time, I didn't know how to report him, so I quit writing to him after I copied the information, pasted it in an email and sent it to him. A year later on a different website, I received a new message from him. Just for the heck of it, I responded to see if he would remember the email address. He didn't. He sent the exact same letter as before, but without the names of the girls who died.

Number 2—The second man who turned out to be a scammer was quite good-looking and ten years younger than me. He lived in Orland Hills, Illinois, near Chicago, according to his profile. He did not ask for my email right away, and there were no red flags for a while. His letters were well written, and we had a very good conversation. They were very different from any I received from other men, and I liked him. I was suspicious from the start, however, wondering just how long it would be before he asked me for money. He sounded too good to be true, and the red flags slowly began to appear. I was curious to see how long it would take for him to ask for money, and I wondered what the emergency would be. It took two weeks.

Robert claimed to be the chief engineer in charge of a submarine headed for the Southeast Highlands to make a delivery of goods. He could not tell me his exact location or the destination for security reasons. He wrote that he liked my profile and my photos and claimed the age difference did not concern him as it was just a number. He was fifty-nine to my seventy-five (age difference is a red flag).

Sun 2/19/2017 9:17 AM

"Good morning S___,

Thank you for your warm reply and hope you had a lovely night rest? It felt really nice reading from you once again and I really do appreciate you sharing so much about yourself and family with me. I am glad you are a dedicated Christian and can't wait to watch you sing. Will be nice to teach you golfing myself as I love golfing and good at it. I have opened and read your latest correspondence at least four times and am in a quandary of emotions as to exactly how to reply? I like to keep my personal life private and I hope I won't regret it as I will be sharing so much with you than I have actually shared with anyone else in my entire life. I understand we are just getting to know each other but want you to know that I'm committed to making this work between us as I'm a one woman kinda man. It's okay for you to get to know other people if you want as I don't know how to communicate with a lot of people at a time. I want you to know that my evaluation of the LOVE process has to do with the content of the heart and not physical appearance. I really prefer being with someone matured as I cannot stand the drama with young people. I like the conception of inner beauty revealed through someones eyes as character is worth more than age and physical appearance. I believe that good things come in smaller packages and you are a total package to me.

I loved everything about your profile and what you've said about yourself so far in your email. I really want us to get all the introduction stuff out of the way soon and get to the good part. I am far from perfect as I know there are no perfect people but working towards perfection is always worth the effort. The more you know about a person the better I like it. The more you want to know about me "I am delighted". If I could hold your attention and find you truly engaged then that's a home run. We could never tell each other too much about ourselves… have absolutely nothing to hide or be ashamed of. I for one have always preferred taking the high road…it's the only direction I know. Also I have a life philosophy that no matter what "I will never let anyone change who I am or try to change anyone". I have worked long and hard to always be "ME".

I'm originally from Orland Hills, IL as that is were my root lies. I was born in IL but had most of my growing up in Europe as my father was a cooperate business man. I was a single child without siblings. My mother was Italian and my father was an American (both parents passed a long time ago). I was a scholar athlete in high school earning 8 varsity letters. I moved to the US With my folks when in was 16. My dads work took him around the world so we moved a lot while growing up. My father was transferred to Buenos Aires, Argentina. He was a corporate business. We were there for almost 7 years. We were then transferred to Spain, lived just outside of Madrid for shy of 3 years before being transferred back to Milan Italy where I lived for 5 years until I graduated from high school. I returned to the US for college in upstate NY. It has been an interesting life, I loved the opportunities to travel and see the world and experience other cultures. The downside, and maybe that's not the right word… is a transient life. My friends growing up were all in similar situations, their fathers were either corporate, military or oil – so people come into your life and then they go, it was all I knew. The only family I have left is an old Aunt in Milan and we are not very close.

I have to say you are certainly in your own right one impressive, accomplished, attractive, amazing woman S____. One of my best qualities is that I am an excellent listener. That's how I acquire new knowledge. Also comes from my upbringing being told that I should be seen and not heard. Talking about my late wife, God gave me in her everything I could have hoped for and more. Then unexpectedly after much suffering and heartache he took her from me (she did not want to leave me)! She was also a professional woman with a stellar reputation who taught me so much and loved me unconditionally to the ump degree! No worries...I already made a pack with myself that I will never compare!!!! Moving forward will be a new dimension in my life. Being in a distant relationship is not for the weak and fickle minded but for the strong who has tons of love to pour out and give across miles to that special someone. If the heart is willing it would definitely find a million ways. I own a four bedroom custom and tastefully built condominium in Orland Hills, IL hosting an outdoor pool, gym, a car park for two cars, one of mine and one of hers but the rest I think we could park outside. I have worked hard to afford me the kind of life I'm living.

I also own a four bedroom condo in Dallas, TX which is also custom built, well furnished and tastefully built hosting an indoor pool, outdoor pool, good lighting system, car park for 3 cars, 2 of mine and 1 of hers. I also own a vacation home in Italy with a taste of the art furnishing as I did make some recent renovations. I love to keep my homes clean at all times. I am financially stable as have been successful for a very long time hence affording and maintaining these properties has never been a problem. I'm pretty open to relocate for the right woman and for the right reasons.

I am a man who is looking for a woman that I can love with everything I have and so far. I want to give my best to a partner and while doing so continue to want to do better because I want to love the woman in my life completely and be loved by her the same way. I want to feel for her in 5 years, 10 years, 19 year into our relationship the same way I felt about her the first time she kissed me. In turn I want to walk into the room where she is and have her come to me and never look away until she reaches me and when she does, I want to have her attention for the rest of the night. I don't care if that happens while we are out in public place or at someone's party or if we are at home on a stormy Friday night. I want a woman who would love and respect me for who I am, that likes to hold my hand and surprise me with a little kiss when I least expect it, or give me a wink from across the room to let me know she's thinking about me or give me a call just to let me know she's thinking about me because I will be doing the same. I want my partner and I to complement each other. I want to add to the relationship and not monopolize it or be secondary to it. I love intimacy with my mate, public displays of affection are fine, touching, caressing, kissing, holding hands, making her smile and laugh, looking deeply into her eyes, making her feel important because she is. I don't know and can't tell if that special person is you but I believe time will tell. I promise to make my one and only the most happiest woman on earth if only she's willing to accept me as part of her. I will be there whenever she needs me and promise never to do anything to hurt her feeling.

As I meet people along the way in life, I have made a life commitment to always leave people better than I met them. If we try, we often leave better ourselves for knowing them! I hope this wasn't too much information… I guess it took almost 59 years to get to this place, how can I sum it up in a few paragraphs! I am usually not this serious, but it feels nice to reflect on my journey, thanks for making it so easy for me to express myself and all I feel! I would like to stop here for now. I would love to have your cell phone number so I can text and call you if you don't mind. Would be looking forward to read from you soon. You are in my thoughts. Hugs and Smiles,

Tue 2/21/2017 10:52 AM

Good Morning, Thoughts of you like threads of gold Keep running through my mind. You are the sweetest person, So gentle and so kind. The beauty of our friendship Fills my heart with joy; The bond that we now share, No other can destroy. Since we embarked on this journey, We've shared so many things, Thoughts, dreams and desires, Hopes on outstretched wing. Our friendship I will treasure Forever and a day, And so sweet thoughts of you Are never far away. Thanks for thinking about me so often as I haven't been able to stop thinking about you also and all the ways I want my love to show. when I love, that special person automatically comes in front of my line. She would always come before anything and anyone else in my life as the only way I know how to love is to love with all of my heart. I want you to know that I'm not communicating with anyone else as I have the conviction in my heart that we are meant for more. I want to share in your good times and bad times and I hope you can come to me whenever something is bothering you. I want you to know that I'm committed towards making this relationship a success and I hope we can both give in our all towards making this relationship a success. I dearly miss having that feminine presence in the house. Nothing would make me happier than watching the sunrise on your face every morning. I believe "Happiness is not a destination, it is a journey and I'm willing to embark on this journey with you. A journey of a lifetime.

I really enjoyed reading your answers to the questions as they brought out the fact once again that we really do share so many similar thoughts. It has really been a wonderful journey getting to know you and the beautiful personality you carry and I intend to continue on this journey for as long as it leads. You such a beautiful person both on the inside and outside Shelby and I really wanna know all there is to know about you. What makes you tick, makes you happy, makes you whine, makes you sad and most importantly what made you the kind of woman you are… You possess all the qualities and good traits I ever desired in a woman and we agree on so many things. I find myself thinking about you constantly Shelby. You should know that you not the only one craving this intensely as I feel exactly the way you do also and definitely wanna see the glass over flowing.

Well, let me give answers to my questions also

1.   What do you do for fun? For fun, I enjoy the outdoors, especially the beach. I love the warmth of the beach but a pair of jeans and warm sweater make for a great day in the Fall as well! Walking on the beach at night, waves crashing restlessly, a million stars in the sky, ahhh perfect for me. I am a lover of travel and exploration of new things. It can be as simple as getting the car and exploring the different historical districts, to a overnight trip to a lake or winery. I think time in a car as a couple is a really special, intimate time. Great music, holding hands and anticipating our adventure together—romance! I also love to hop on a plane and see a new state or country. I enjoy golfing or just yachting and cruising the vast mass of the sea. I think I'm ready to own one once I retire. I like dining out, plays, see a beautiful work of art. I'm pretty flexible as far as activities. I like going to the

movies or theater, hanging out with friends, sharing jokes, listening to music and also spending time with someone interesting. On a quieter note, I miss lazy mornings in bed with someone to snuggle with or the Sundays when you get up, start your day and decide—heck with it, let's go back to bed!

2. What are some of your inexpensive gift to give? One of my inexpensive gift to give is my time as its very special to me. I also love to give candles and a coupon for a romantic evening, sunflowers, a card that express my feelings, flowers, a nice bottle of perfume (Chanel No. 5) is my favorite for my woman. I love outing with my woman and shopping together. I also love to snuggle up with a glass of wine and a movie, nice dinner with candles, picnic at the park, cuddling under a blanket and watching a romantic movie and I sure love to give nice piece of jewelries to my woman as gifts although that becomes a little expensive but it's a nice thing to do when you are with the right person.

3. What are your favorite meals and seafood? Love all foods and love to try new foods. Love Mexican food, pasta, lobster, Italian and I'm open to try new places and things. I appreciate a great restaurant, but I do not believe that fancy necessarily means great!! I avoid chain restaurants if possible—for the everyday, I eat to live (pretty healthy and lean choices) BUT, I do think that food is about pleasure, so if you behave 90% of the time and are active, you should be able to really enjoy all the great food that is out there! I LOVE to cook though I have nobody to cook for! As an empty nester, I do not get much of a chance to cook, but when I do, I am in heaven!

4. Whats your favorite color? I love bright colors also such as yellow, blue, orange, green but wear more of black when I need to be very professional. I also love black when it comes to cars. I drive a 2014 Wangler Jeep, a 2015 Mercedes S65 AMG, and a 2014 BMW M7. Thinking of getting an Audi R8. I think they call it having an adrenaline foot as I love to race and speed but know when to respect speed limits except when I'm on the freeway.

5. Do you love flowers and which is your favorite? What is not to love about any flower? Roses, lilies, lilacs, tulips, peony, lavender and daisies. I like them, but I think a bouquet of fresh roses, lilac, peony or daisies from the garden top them all! However, for your reference, I am a single stem kind of man– simple and beautiful wins my heart.

6. What are your favorite movies? Love comedy, action movies, sci-fi movies and some old soul romance movies like sweet home Alabama, princess bride, when harry met sally, gone with the wind, you've got mail, the wedding singer, the notebook, sleepless in Seattle, pretty woman, dirty dancing, 6 days 7 nights, the list can go on. I also love to read good books.

7. What are your favorite songs you love to listen to? I love western music, country music, love songs, 70's and 80's. I recently started listening to John Legend, and Ed Sheeran. I think they are nice. I like Adele too and love anything by Barry White. When a man loves a woman by Michael Bolton, anything by Celine Dion, my best friend by Tim McGraw, Toby Keith, Neil Diamond, Bob Seger's "you will accompany me" A bit of contemporary Gospel like "It's your love" by Tim McGraw and Faith Hill and the list could keep

going. I can dance for days listening to good music. I also love live Orchestra and live performing arts and also feel classical music is great.

8. What are your expectations in a relationship? My greatest expectation in a relationship is faithfulness and honesty because if you have both, the love you share will be so strong and lasting and all other things will just follow. I want to be with someone who loves me, not just me but who wants to share the everyday life with me, talk about everything and who helps me be a better person. I don't know how to holler or fight and have a rule of never going to bed angry.

9. What are your greatest fear? My biggest fear in a relationship is that it grow stale or lose its passion and intimacy. I think many couples take love for granted, they put children, work and others in front of being lovers and before they know it's too late. I want to have a lifetime relationship and I know I can find someone who feels as I do if I haven't found her already. Love, passion, respect are too important to me to settle. I also fear dishonesty which would hurt my heart. I think I could deal with anything else. I am a very trusting person and I absolutely hate (I use that word rarely) lying and deceit. 10. If you had three wishes, what would they be? First wish would be for world peace where we wouldn't have to live in fear or send soldiers out to their early graves mostly over political interest and trying to protect the country and making it safer for people to live… Next would be for a very big and happy family full of laughter and merriment with the right woman by my side whom I can share all the love I have in me with… Last wish would be to live a long and happy life full of excitement and contentment.

I would stop here for now and leave a couple more questions.

Here are some more questions.

1. How important is it to you to be faithful?
2. What is the first thing you noticed about me?
3. Would you say you have a "type"? Do I fit what you thought you were looking forming lovers?
4. Do you believe in soul mates? What about love at first sight? What about friends becoming lovers?
5. What's your idea of a perfect first date?
6. Do you consider yourself the jealous type?
7. Do you think we're compatible?
8. Do you see us having a future together?
9. Are you into "public displays of affection"?
10. What makes you laugh? What makes you angry?
11. What are your relationship goals?
12. Are you comfortable discussing finances with your partner?13. How far can you go for your partner? Sending you all the warmth of my heart and you can trust that I'm gonna be wearing a smile on my face till I read from you again. Will be looking forward to your message. Hope your night was as beautiful as a Cupid. Hugs and kisses," ~~

M

Wed 2/22/2017 7:04 PM

My dearest S____, It is so very obvious you are so polished, educated and charming you run circles around me and leave me totally speechless and in a state of euphoria. All I can do is sit back and absorb the full beauty of your being. You have become a part of me. I have never known anyone quite like you. Each day I awake, my first lucid thought is "Will I hear from Shelby today"? What beautiful thought will she greet me with? Will her feelings be deeper than the day before? I anticipate every next mail and text from you. I want you to know that I am totally embedded in your existence. I am definitely without any question of doubt "falling in love with you". It is as complicated as it is simple!!! I am not flighty or insane. I am mature...been around quite awhile and know love from infatuation. This is "LOVE"! I feel it every time I write or read from you. If it feels right, it is right. I believe the rainbow carried all our wishes for the future. Our pasts will not interfere with the present. The presents is ours to have, mold and embrace... the past will not tarnish that in any way. Our senses are focused on nurturing and building our tomorrow. This will be a new dimension in life. You and I together are now a blank canvas on which we are going to paint our own dynamic picture...it will be unique, beautiful, individual, aesthetic in every way... it will be our "Love Story"!!!! I will give it my all and my best to be worthy of your love and full acceptance. You are so articulate...it just re-enforces how deep and intelligent you are which is such a turn on to me....I love intelligent women and you definitely fill that requirement. I am so impressed with you and everything you emulate. You are to me a TOTAL PACKAGE.

My interest goes beyond the outside wrapping. I have known individuals that are stunning on the outside but miserable on the inside...not worth the time of day. I believe once a person matures you get past the hang up with looks. I'm glad we really do enjoy a lot of the same things and can't wait for us to be together. . . . I am always on call here as most of the workers reports to me and I am in charge of any mechanical accident here. I suggested Lady Gaga's song because I love what the song portray. If you hurt me I will always try to make a better us because I know there is a million reason I have to keep us together. Nothing would make me happier than seeing all of our dreams fulfilled together. All I want from you is to take good care of yourself as I want you to be in the best of health when I'm with you as we have so much to explore together. . .

There's nothing I want more than to focus on you and the beautiful thoughts we share together. Everyday I draw closer to you because you never cease to amaze me and draw me closer. These past couple days has really helped in knowing more about ourselves and what we desire in a partner. Your words sends messages and chills down my spine. I really can't wait to meet you and start spending time together. I know you must be looking very beautiful with your new hair but will always care for you and love you Shelby. Your mom was a successful woman and hope we will always keep communication when you away? As you know already I hate missing you. I guess I owe you some answers to the last questions I asked.

1. How important is it to you to be faithful? It is the most important factor for me – it is completely intertwined with truthfulness and honesty. If I cannot trust there is no relationship… It is the fundamental and bedrock of every relationship, without it, all else will fail…I can't imagine being in a relationship without communication. Both parties have to work together and stimulate each other in various ways to spice up the relationship. It shouldn't be a job for a particular person but a shared obligation to always watch out for each other…Discussing your fears with your partner is sure a step ahead as there is hardly a problem without solution and if you can just open up about anything, then I believe couples would always have an understanding and even stand stronger as they work to overcome those fears together….I'm very modern but some of my morals are old fashioned. Within the closed relationship with my woman there are no barriers, no restrictions, no prudishness. I'm

loyal, can keep secrets and I'm private about family, couple and intimate things.

2. What is the first thing you noticed about me? I was very much impressed with your charm and awesome personality. There was a gentle look and loving eyes upon your face. I go by feelings and vibes a lot and to me you gave off the energy of a smart, kind humanistic woman. All the qualities I admire. I did not feel negative or controlling energies from you yet knew at the same time you could be counted on. Would protect your man, family and all that is yours. I could see all I ever desired in a woman in you and if I had met you in person, I would have gazed into your beautiful eyes…I am an "eye contact" type of person…next I would have listened to your tender and caring voice….after that I would have given you a hug and a tender kiss because touch is so important.

3. Would you say you have a "type"? Do I fit what you thought you were looking for? Well, I do not think I have a type per se… All I want in a woman is a woman of good character and humble nature and I'm glad there was still one left. I am seeking someone who can communicate on all levels… physically, emotionally and spiritually…I am seeking someone who is caring and not afraid to share herself with others. Seeking someone who is honest and trustworthy… I was attracted by your good sense of humor, distinguished character and kind words. Yes, I do believe from what we have shared thus far, you possess all of these qualities. I believe women are God's gift to men and they deserved to be treated with care, loved, their opinion respected and they should be well taken care of. Their voice deserves to

be heard as they sometimes see farther than we men actually see…I know you are God's gift to me.

4.   Do you believe in soul mates? What about love at first sight? What about friends becoming lovers? Yea I believe in soul mates who stands for and compliments each other. Who are always there for each other through thick and thin. I know I can find someone with those same core values and traits that would be a perfect fit for me and I want to spend the rest of my life making her happy. I believe we should make the most of what we have. I also believe in twin flames. I believe in reincarnation and believe souls come back to be together to love but often there is a higher deeper mission and purpose. That is true love to highest degree. I also do believe in love at first site. It does happen though it has never happened to me. My love develops over time with good and steady communication which is happening for us already… Getting to know more about each other. I've met people who never seemed appealing to me but felt differently about them after having some good interaction with them… I absolutely do not believe in nor partake in one night stands or "I do not know your name sex" I need the connection and personal commitment to make love. Looks can be deceiving as there is nothing so deceptive as one's outward appearance. Is like buying a house because of the paint when you never know what's inside the house. Friends becoming lovers? Friendship must be a good foundation for a true "love" relationship…so yes, I see friends becoming lovers. Lovers should be best friends…there for one another through "good and bad" times, sorrowful and joy-filled days…I believe its actually the best combination because then

they really share and understand each other and fit together in all ways.

5.   Whats your idea of a perfect first date? My idea of a perfect first date would be picking up my lady in a very nice and fancy car and taking her to the most beautiful restaurant ever. Somewhere quiet were we can have a private or candle light dinner. Its a time to feel connection and be able to laugh together. Get to talk over a glass of soft wine. A walk after dinner, holding hands…do some star and moon gazing…. and a gentle kiss to say good night!

6.   Do you consider yourself the jealous type? No I don't consider myself a jealous type. If I love, I trust fully and know they will respect and honor our relationship. Jealousy is being insecure and not believing in your woman and it leads to always being suspicious and anxious. It cannot exist in a true relationship because it ruins it.

7.   Do you think we are compatible? Judging from our emails and conversations, I would say Yes. We are both open people with deep ideas and morals who love life and who want to share with a mate in all aspects to the fullest. Although we come from different roots, we are both broad minded and our life experiences have made us accepting and yet we both know what we want and go for it without being selfish. We seem to enjoy a lot of the same things and value the time it takes to build a strong relationship. We both are kind-hearted, gentle people, who value communication and physical affection. We both value our faith and God. We are both hopeful to find an endless and abiding love.

8. Do you see us having a future together? Yea I do and I believe it will take some work, some logistical planning, faith in uncharted waters…some of these tasks we have already started. Will be a new journey for us…But I believe we might just be up for the challenge. If we truly want it and are committed to getting to know each other more and more. At same time, often the heart has a mind of its own which goes beyond logic. It's not foolish. If it feels right it is right.

9. Are you into "public displays of affection"? Yea I do. I love to hold hands…receive a tender kiss on the sidewalk or in the park. I would love to give a gentle brush of my hand across your cheek, a special look in your eyes or smile on your face that only I can interpret. I want to share my love in a manner of respectful display so the public would think us well and be happy to see it. Want the world to see how strong and beautiful our love is together and be jealous because it is reciprocal.

10. What makes you laugh? Playfulness of my partner…. something silly done by accident. A good comedy, a theater movies stand up comics. Seeing the natural beauty of nature and universe. Listening to small children explaining things to one another because kids also do the magic. Their little and tender ways makes me laugh thinking they are doing something right and yet they are doing a complete opposite… Like when they take you pictures and you found out the only body part that shows is either your head or just you nose and eye. Lol. They are wonderful people to have…

11. What makes me angry? I don't easily get angry at people and always try to avoid a confrontation that

would make me angry. I'm slow to anger but can't help but get angry when I ask for help and its refused. Lies and cheats, stupid politics and laws.

12. What are your relationship goals? I wish to rebuild my life and once again share fully and completely my life with one special woman. To love that special woman more than I love her the previous day, share everything together, marry her and make her the happiest woman in the world, give her everything she desires, grow old together. There would never be a dull moment as she will always be appreciated and also receive same in return. I am not looking for casual flings. I want to share all moments happy and sad, want to be there in all aspects for them and receive same in return. Shelby I am happy you are that special woman.

13. Are you comfortable discussing finances with your partner? Yes in a closed loving relationship I feel there should be no secrets, illusions in things done, spent, invested etc There should be joint decisions. Two heads are better than one. I want to share everything I have with that special woman. I'm thankful for all God has blessed me with in the past and present that when I retire I don't plan on working anymore as I have all I've ever wanted and desired in life except someone special to spend the rest of my life with but now I have you Shelby. I believe in sharing as long as one party does not take advantage of the other. At our age, we each come with hard earned wealth whatever it may be and it is only right that to a great extent especially in beginning have control and say over our assets. We cannot take it with us so should enjoy as long as we can to no extremes. I believe in helping and sharing with those in need as long as it's

real and not forced or abused. I am very comfortable discussing my finances with you if you are willing to listen. I hope you would never be shy to ask me anything. Thank you for opening up to me about you renting or buying a house maybe we could buy a house together if is okay with you.

14. How far are you willing to go for your partner? Fully in all aspects. To the ends of the earth and to deepest depth of the ocean. I would stand by her side, believe and honor her. I would not use or betray her. I would love and protect her with all that I am and all that I have and do anything possible to help in a situation.

Somethings about me, I may have said some of this before but it belongs here now: I love to sit in the sun, walk on a beach and carrying up a good conversation with a nice glass of wine is high on my list especially if that occurs in a place for adults. I enjoy doing anything adult once in awhile. There is nothing tangible that I want, it is the intangible that excites me. Don't get me wrong, I like nice things as much as anyone else and I enjoy the things that money can buy, but things and places can feel empty when you are alone. I love life. I know that the important things in life are things that touch your heart, bring the greatest joys and possibly even greater pain at times. I am looking to share those joyous moments with someone special, someone who would help me carry the sorrows we will have to weather and I think I just might have found her. I don't need fancy, I need honesty, sharing, caring, love, happiness and many, many laughs. I am down to earth, believe in God and believe that strong relationships take commitment and work to keep them fresh. I am a loyal, supportive partner who believes that special person is always first, we hold tightly together by love, not always blood.

I am glad I could make you find yourself again. I love all what you have said about your meaning of I LOVE YOU. You don't need t search anymore because you have me now Shelby. You answers are similar to mine and will always appreciate you for you being yourself. I am a bit tired but will try to make my meaning of I love you short as you have explained it all but will add some points.

Inspired wealth, Listen to each other, open your heart, value our union, Express our trust, yield to good sense, Overlook mistakes and Understand the differences. believe with this you will understand we have more similarities than you thought. Please make me believe I am the only man in your life now as I am worried of getting hurt. It took me a long time to be myself again after the death of my wife. I am already at the stage of no return with you and there is no turning back for me. I would stop here for now babe as duty calls and would be looking forward to read from you soon. Sending you lots of hugs and kisses,

Lovingly,

To summarize, Robert seemed to be an excellent writer whose grammar and spelling were quite good. There are several red flags though as he writes: he was a self-employed professional traveling outside of the US; he professed love for me almost immediately, sending love letters with cute images and links to his favorite love songs; he told me to stop communicating with others on the dating site so we could concentrate on each other; he was irritated with me when I told him I would not fall in love with anyone I had not met in person; he did not like my answer to his question about whether I "loved unconditionally" or not; he ignored most of the questions I asked him; and a background search said he could not be found. It took two weeks for the emergency to take place, and that became the norm. Robert's emergency was an explosion in the engine room, which caused the submarine to be "dead in the water." For some reason, his credit cards would not work, and he needed me to purchase an expensive part to fix the engine and send it to him by seaplane. The part cost twenty thousand dollars, and he became very upset with me when I told him I did not have that kind of money. He attempted to make me feel guilty by telling me he was afraid the pirates would attack and kill him and his crew and steal his shipment. He even became verbally abusive before I finally came to my senses, realizing that I did not have to listen to him and blocked him!

Number 3—Up until this point, I had managed to keep my wits about me and did not yield to these first two attempted scams. What was it about Eugene that caused me to lower my defenses and send him some money? That is a very good question. But before telling his story, here is what was going on in my life at that particular time: I was emotionally a wreck as I finally had a buyer for my Tennessee house and was packing for my move to Michigan. I was alone in the house that my husband and I had designed and built. We had lived there seventeen years. I had made an offer to buy a house in Michigan and was waiting for the sellers to agree to my price. It depressed me to be selling my beautiful Tennessee home and leaving all the friends and a part-time job I enjoyed. My mother had passed away five weeks earlier. Needless to say, I was stressed, sad, lonely, extremely vulnerable, and I was sick!

The second day after I arrived in Tennessee to finish packing up for the big move, I began to feel very ill. I went first to a walk-in clinic where I was tested for the flu and strep throat. My temperature was 103°. The PA decided I had a sinus infection and gave me a prescription for ____. Three days later, I did not feel any better, and my fever had climbed to 105°. I went to my former doctor who said it was the flu. The third week, I started for Florida for a vacation with my daughter, and I was still sick. The third doctor said it was strep throat and gave me a different antibiotic. Finally, twenty-four hours later, I began to feel better.

Back to the scamming incident. I started to chat with Eugene before I left for Tennessee because I wanted to find a friend, and his profile said he lived within ten miles of me. In our very first message, he wrote that he was leaving the very next day for China on a buying trip. This was going to be his last trip before retirement and would be back in two weeks. Within a few days, I received the message that he was in trouble. He had finished buying the items he needed, and while his purchases were being loaded onto the ship for America, a Chinese dockworker had fallen from up high on the ship. He was hurt badly and had died. Eugene had been questioned by the police, who requested to see his passport. They took it with them along with his money and some other documents he had with him. They had told him they would give them back when they finished their investigation. Eugene's story unfolded over several days. The police told him he would have to pay the dead man's hospital bills, and after the man died, Eugene was going to have to pay for the funeral and a sum of money to make up for the family's loss of income from his job.

Eugene wrote that his family and friends had come up with most of the money, but he needed more. He was starving since the police had kept all his money. This man seemed to be in very serious trouble, and every day, the situation got worse. It sounded like the stories I had read in which Americans had been detained in foreign countries, and I really felt sorry for this man. He was trapped in a foreign country and starving to death. He asked me for a loan and promised to pay me back as soon as he got home. I was exhausted and ill, and against my better judgment, I wired him some money. It wasn't enough, and he begged for more. All my things were now in a truck, and I was alone again driving to Michigan, and this guy is dying of starvation in China! I was a mess!

When I got back to Michigan, I was so upset about this poor man, and so I shared the story with my daughter, asking her if there was any way they could help this poor man. That was when she told me I had been scammed! At first I did not believe it, but she took me to the Michigan State Police station in the morning, and I made a report. The trooper told there was nothing that could be done about it and that my money was gone.

I felt embarrassed and humiliated. I had not wanted to tell my daughter or my friends that I had been so stupid, but I had to talk to somebody. Everyone was concerned about me, but I would never forget how embarrassed and humiliated I was. I try to put the whole thing behind me, but the subject pops up time and again, and I remember and am humiliated all over again. I even have begun to feel like I am the criminal instead of the victim.

Surfing the internet about a year after this happened, I saw Eugene's photo again on a different dating site. Cold chills ran down my spine, and the hair on my arms stood straight up! I felt like I had seen a ghost. His photo and profile were exactly the same; not a word had been changed. I finally announced loudly, "Well, isn't it wonderful that you made it back to the USA without my money." I screamed at my computer, "You jerk! I wonder how you got out of China without my money?" Then I reported him on the website. I never liked him anyway! I just felt sorry for him.

Number 4—The minute I saw the photo of this handsome man requesting my friendship on Facebook, I fell, and I fell hard! His name was Charles, and he was absolutely the most handsome man I had ever seen! I accepted his request even though I knew I shouldn't. His response was immediate, and we texted back and forth for at least an hour. He said all the right words I needed to hear, and it was fun to chat with him. I received his message about the time I started chatting with Eugene, and so I was in Tennessee. I was ill, lonely, and vulnerable. He really cared about me, it seemed.

After settling the scam with Eugene, my daughter asked who else I was chatting with, and I had to confess I was chatting with Charles and one other man. I told her he was the one that I thought I was in love with. I simply would not believe that he was also a scammer. My son-in-law went on the internet and turned up an article about the oil rig scammers! None of the things Charles had told me about his job were the truth, so I blocked him.

✦

Number 5—Maynard said he was a jewelry designer with businesses in Atlanta, Georgia, and Beverly Hills, California. Maynard did not fit the profile of a scammer and did not exhibit the red flags of a scammer. He even initiated "Skyping" sessions with me. The only red flag was that he fell in love with me and wanted to come to Michigan to meet me. Because of the scam with Eugene, I was forced to stop chatting with Maynard. About six months later, he texted me and asked to borrow $100 for some medicine he needed. I felt very badly for him but told him I couldn't, and he said that he understood, and we said goodbye. I felt terrible, but what else could I do?

✦

Number 6—Charley from Chicago, Illinois, had a master's degree in engineering and was a construction manager. He sent me a nice photo of himself with his sixteen-year-old son. He told me he had been badly hurt when his wife had left him, but he was finally ready to move on, and I was the one he wanted. His mother lived with him and took care of his son in his absence.

A background search on him showed a person of that name in Arizona where Charley said he owned a second home. However, his emails and messages were filled with red flags. I met him on eHarmony, and a few days after we began chatting, I received a message from eHarmony informing me that Charley's account had been terminated because of fraud. I forwarded the message to Charley, who replied that he didn't know why some people had been telling lies about him, and he hoped I would love him enough to believe him and trust him. He was innocent, he said, and wanted desperately for me to believe him.

However, there were too many red flags against him. He owned his own construction company and had just won the contract for a job in Egypt. He had to leave right away, and although he had said we would meet before he left, there was not enough time. He had to leave immediately but would return in a few weeks, and then we would meet and, hopefully, get married. Soon after landing in Egypt, however, a large piece of equipment broke, and he needed me to wire him some money as soon as possible. I blocked him.

About a year later, I decided to see if he would answer the phone, so I called him, and he answered. He immediately asked me if I had his money yet. I ended the call and blocked his number again. I was no longer curious! I certainly was not interested in chatting with this creep!

Number 7—Besides the group of scammers pretending to work on an oil rig, there are also those who pretend they are in the United States military and are serving their country in a foreign country. I have received messages from five or six guys from this group. Two of them wrote very suggestive messages, and I blocked them right away. Two more seemed nice, but they did ask me to chat with them on Google Hangout instead of the chatroom on the dating website. I chatted with them for a while until one day I saw that I could check a military website for names of all men and women who have served their country. I looked up the two names these guys gave and discovered their names on the list. However, they were listed as deceased. What a shame that men who gave their lives in the service to their country are now victims of scammers!

The following message is a phishing template:

> Hello, this is S. . ., I'm sorry for just getting back to you. I got a message from you on the dating website. The website seems to be no luck for me, and I have been out

of town for vacation. Also, I don't get notifications on new messages from the site in a very long time, that way – I missed getting back to you. Now, I'd like to know more about you too. I had to renew my membership just to get your address and requested for a cancellation. Please get back to me. You seem to be courteous and I really like your profile. Please, I really want to get to know more about you and let's find out where the chemistry takes us. You can follow here to check my profile on the dating site. Regards, S. . .".

The following words have appeared in several different messages I have received and are definitely sent by a scammer. If you see these words in any of your messages, beware.

My late wife was a loving woman before she met her untimely death. . . now intending to move on with my life with that lovely, honest, faithful woman with so much love to give because I am tired of public settings with dishonest, unfaithful People.

I have even received copies of a passport with the name of the person who sent it and a stamp with the date and country in which he said he was presently working. This was sent to prove to me that he was telling me the truth. However, he was *not*!

CHAPTER TWENTY-THREE

Love(?) Letters

Since there are so many people who say they cannot understand how another adult could be taken in by a scammer, I am including some the following messages and emails from two different men (supposedly) to show how beautifully worded they are (especially the second one) and for all to see that they are exactly what a lonely, vulnerable woman would want to read from a lover. They remind me of some of the romance novels I have read and I knew they were too perfect to be true, but that didn't stop me from wishing that the second one might be real, and, why I couldn't wait for morning to read what he had written. It made me feel good to read these words at a time when I was very lonely and vulnerable.

There are a few red flags to be spotted in the letters, but neither man ever asked me for money, and both of them suddenly stopped writing to me and I was left hanging.

On June 3, 2018, James wrote the following:

> Hello, dear. . . I'm not quite sure what I'm supposed to tell a complete stranger. But here goes nothing. Your beautiful and you were something. What matters in life is who you are and what you're doing with your life. Made mistakes? Redeem them live the good life so far continue to do it. Don't let people bring you down or make you feel

worthless because they are far from right. After viewing your profile, I got so impressed that I have to send you this message just to indicate my genuine interest as I was encouraged to try the dating site by my mom who is tired of seeing me lonely of which I was finally signed up by my daughter. I am well-balanced, listen well, young at heart, funny, love to laugh, have healthy sense of humor, patient, financially secured, genuine, independent, show passion, honest, and can be trusted. I enjoy a variety of things to do and always like to experience other opportunities. I love the beach so much and it's always fun to walk in the cold beach sand barefooted. I will have to say that the high agent my profile is a mistake as my daughter made an error when registering me on the site of which I could not figure out how to fix the age issues. So, I am a healthy 64 years old man and I do not believe that age or distance is a barrier to a loving relationship as what matters most is the love and beauty inside.

Of course, I would really love to get to know you well and also tell you more about myself as I want you to feel free to write me directly to my direct email contact:_____ or you can send me your own email contact as for me to write you first if that is what you want. Why I am giving my email to you is because I am not regular on this site as I am not too familiar with the social media knowing that I am old-school type of person and hope to meet after a couple of emails. I hope to hear from you soon enough so that we can open direct communication and get to know each other better. Wishing you all the very best at the moment. . . Cheers! Kind regards. J____

James's profile photo was of an attractive businessman wearing a white shirt and a red tie and sitting at his desk in an office. A nearby filing cabinet had VW sticker on the side. It looked very official to me.

The only red flag is in the last paragraph where he asks for my email address so quickly. I asked myself, "Wow, is this guy for real? Be still, my heart." There is no way to tell if "James" is this person's real name or if the photo is of the guy writing to me. But I wrote, "Hey There :-)"

James replied immediately. "Hey how r u. Nice to have you here."

As we continued to chat, however, several red flags began to appear as follows:

> Construction business. He had just won a contract in a foreign country. He was leaving the next day. He has a young daughter. He asked me to move to another website for our conversation. This was his last job as he was going to retire when he came back to the USA.

I suspected James was a scammer when he wrote that he had won a contract in Taiwan, so l tried to speed up the process by writing, "You have to think about a lot of things. I hope you are prepared for all emergencies."

He responded, "Honestly I am doing the very best. I heard Taiwan is a difficult country. And I am preparing as much as I can."

I wrote, "So many things can happen unexpectedly and you may need several thousand dollars extra just in case."

His reply was, "Hey S___, what makes you this beautiful woman you are? I so admire and want the very best for you . . . what can I ever do to make you happy for the rest of you life?"

James and I corresponded for several weeks, and he shared his challenges at work: he couldn't get enough workmen to do the job, there were problems in obtaining the required materials, etc. He was becoming exhausted, and he wrote less and less. He finally stopped writing altogether. I don't know what happened to him. Was he just wanting my attention? Was he going to ask for money? Maybe he just wanted a pen pal. I do not know. There is even the possibility that he became one of several scammers since this incident. Who knows?

◊

On July 22, 2018, I received the first message from Alex. He stayed on the website's platform and did not ask for my email address right away, nor did he suggest moving to another platform. In fact, we chatted for a week before he finally asked for my email address. He said he wanted to write longer letters because he had to confess that although he had wanted to take things slowly, he found himself thinking about me all the time and thought he was falling in love with me.

As I write this, it has been five weeks since he first sent me a message, and he has not yet mentioned an emergency or requested money. We have talked on the phone twice, and he had no accent, nor did his voice sound unusual or familiar. I am including only a sampling of his letters because they are each three to four pages long or more, and I hope you can begin to understand how a lonely, vulnerable woman can become taken in by these letters.

Although I have had quite a lot of experience in this subject, I could hardly wait to get out of the bed in the morning to see what he had written each day. I admit that I am guilty of becoming addicted to receiving the attention I get from the dating websites. As I read the letters, I hoped this was the "one." Was Alex a scammer or not? I don't know. He never asked for money, but he certainly had my attention.

This is letter number 5 from Alex, July 27, 2018:

> Hello Dearest, how are you today? I hope this email finds you on a loving mood. I want to thank you for the email and the almighty for giving us another day. I had to wake up this early to send you this email because I have been thinking so much about you and I will be having a very busy day so I need to get this off to you now. Like I said in my first email to you; though I will like to take this relationship slow, I will like to be positive. My giving you my heart at this point does not mean that I am trying to rush it rather I am being positive and consistence so forgive me if it seems that am taking the wrong step. . .

Let me say here that going on line to find a suitable companion seemed hopeless for me at the beginning. Most of my earlier contacts that wrote stating that POF suggested my profile to them as a MATCH were from much younger women so I could not understand how I could be a match to a 37 years old woman when I stated what I wanted on my profile. They always left me feeling bewildered and asking the questions – should I be flattered or insulted? In addition, there was always the concern – "what were the motives"?

My faith was restored, when I decided to write instead of wait to be written; I wrote you and you appeared I thank my "lucky star" and enjoy the wonder of it. Essentially, I was so deeply happy that you displayed the qualities I was looking for. I found out that we shared a lot of the same interests and I adored the expressive e-mails.

When I emailed you, I told you that I looked at your profile for over 30 minutes and you must be wondering what I saw during that 30 minutes that made me email you. I have come to realize that lonely times make us search harder for the good times. Bad times are only vague memories and we can look to the future with optimism to happy times. To "give" and "receive", to pamper, to spoil, to guide, to care for in all ways, makes for a wonderful relationship. There is no need for anger, when there is understanding, loyalty and sincerity, open communication and the ability to compensate for differences. Life is meant to be enjoyed and thus, should not harbor hurtful thoughts and actions. . . They say "Love" overcomes all obstacles. But to love blindly – leaves scares in your heart. The "ups" and "downs" in people's life's can be painful but can be healed with limitless compassion. Mine is healed so let us heal yours if it is still there. If your heart has been damaged too much by some cruel evil man, I can help you fix it like I fixed that of my late wife. If you have lost a partner like me, I can still fix it like I fixed mine or let's say, we can fix ours together. When I say we can fix ours together, I know that Life isn't always a bowl of cherries. Based on this fact, I have decided that I need a woman that is not looking for someone to make her happy, but rather someone to share happiness and experience life's adventures and sometimes tribulations. You will agree with me that everybody need happiness both man and woman. Happiness is created in many ways – mostly in what people do and say! Your words can encourage me to drink long and hard from the cup of life; to capture every drop of adventure that comes my way.

I often ask myself, why we met – even if it was in such an unconventional way! I truly believe that a "path" is mapped out for us, when we are born. Are we given a purpose – are we given instructions on how to live our life and what we are to achieve? We are guided by our parents, teachers and friends and unconsciously adapt some of their ways to our life. However, there is a greater plan for us in the making. We are tested daily to make us stronger. Stumbling blocks are put in our way to overcome and make us rise above them. Many people travel from cradle to grave without ever seeing themselves clearly, without accepting heartache and grief and without ever wondering about their past, present and future. They accept their life blindly, without questions or true understanding of their own value and potential. They become frustrated, disillusioned and bitter. We have all been given the tools to excel, feel more important, more fulfilled and more useful. You have shown me that you know how to use the tools so don't ever let anyone tell you that you will not accomplish and excel at what you have chosen, or perhaps, what had been chosen for you. What measure do they use to compare, or do they feel inadequate in their on achievements?

. . .So, was I meant to come into your life to help you see your own worth, to encourage and support and show you the heights that you have already accomplished. I have not chosen your "path" and don't know the plan decided for you, but I know you have a passion for life, so you are and always will be successful. I am grateful to you for giving me your trust, but I think you now know, I would not misguide you.

When I think about you, a picture comes to mind, a woman sweet and gentle, with a heart that is one of a kind. Your light shines ever bright – your love an endless sea. . . . and nothing could be sweeter than the love you would have for me. I see you as my inspiration, but most of all God's Gift to me". I want to wish you a happy day and with this email welcome you to an inspiring day of good luck and success in all you do. This letter may not be too romantic but inspiring enough to start your day with a new relationship. I thank God above for you. May you always find new blessings for as long as you may live. . . Hugs! Hugs! It's me; Alex"

This is letter number 6, July 29, at ten forty-five in the morning:

I must confess that it was such a joyful and pleasant moment with you on the phone yesterday. Though it was a short conversation for me, but I was actually feeling like a young teenager receiving his first call from his high school girlfriend. . .lol. You sounded pretty tender, smart, and intelligent and most importantly I really enjoyed the fact that we both talked peacefully and laughed together. That alone has showed me that you would be so much fun to be with! I will try to call you today. I want to hear more of your sweet voice, but then again, I can't wait to see you soon

I want you to know that you are presently making me the happiest man on earth again by putting these handsome smiles on my face every morning that I wake up. . . You are always on my mind. . . I want you to know that my day starts when I receive your wonderful e-mail, and ends with me sending you a reply. That is why I do wonder why you are in my thoughts all the time? The in between time is filled with romantic notions, breathless anticipation and a million and one thoughts of how our first meeting will go. Will there be fireworks will there be balloons in the sky? I know I am fantasizing, like a foolish teenager, but it makes me feel young and so extraordinarily happy.

I must confess that I have tried to suppress the feeling of calling you my love all this while to avoid looking like I am rushing everything but each time I want to email you, it keeps coming into my mind. It is a known fact that I am falling seriously in love with you and cannot stand not seeing you soon.

You have brought this change and joy in me that I believe has attracted this lifetime business luck to me. Meeting you brought the breakthrough that I have been struggling to have with the investor for almost two years. All I want you is to understand my situation and take me the way you see me. It's not that I fall in love easily but having been alone for over seven years makes me want you as soon as possible. All that I am sure is that this is not lust or a game of days but a life time relationship. I was married to my wife for 26 happy years and she was my first and only marriage. That alone will tell you more about me. Please bear with me if I use those words so early. It's due to the way I feel that make me write the way I do. You are an angel in disguise. . . . you have touched my heart thus making a difference in my life. Bringing more Joy and success than you will ever know that you have done. . .I think of you every moment of the day and I wish that at the end of a very hectic day that you will be there my side. I need you so much. I want you to know that the first day we knew over the computer, I knew you were the one for me. It is almost two weeks now and we are still fondly in each other's minds, souls, and hearts. Before I met you online, I almost forgot what love really was until my heart truly started aching for you. Each day we are apart, tears ran down my face unconditionally for the longing of you near me. I never knew a woman could have stolen my heart again and made it truly hers. I never knew I could love a woman more than my own life.

I long for the day I can finally look into your beautiful soft, kind eyes and tell you how much I miss you, and need you. What I need to survive and make it through this lonely world can only be conquered with you by my side because it was really a great battle with line during my seven years of loneliness.

I do not think there are any words that could describe the way I actually feel about us. We will plan our meeting before I return back home. All I know is you, Darling you are the only woman that is in my mind, the only woman that is in my soul, the only woman who truly and unconditionally has my heart for my life time and many more lifetimes the world has to offer us.

When I think about you, my eyes start to water because I know you are somewhere else and not in my arms. But the thought of you keeps me going and going for another breath of fresh air to keep my longing for you in my life going. I will never leave, and I will truly never hurt you. . .

I am aware of all your dreams and wishes. We shall accomplish them as great couples. We shall always have the best of time to share together. I have never met someone that is as intelligent as you are in recent years. You are my dream come true. What can I even do without you? Thanks so much for making me fall deeply in love again. You are my perfect match. I hope you are enjoying the new day over there. Darling, I am scared of tonight because am so sure am not going to sleep but think about you always. You are the best thing that has happened to me in recent years and I am very proud of you. I see myself as the luckiest man on earth to have you as my darling and friend. Please thank you so much. Take care"

This is from August 9, 2018:

My Darling, Thank you for your email and your concern over my mother's illness. It has not really been easy for me not being able to communicate with you or at least write you an email. I had to go out to an internet café to be able to send you this email. I couldn't go for two straight days without looking at my email knowing very well that there may be an email from you waiting for me. . . .

I want you to know that I have really missed you and was so happy when I opened my email and there was a mail from you! I can't wait to be with you. I can't wait to look into your beautiful eyes and tell you how much I love you! I can't wait to hug you at the airport! I can wait to touch your face and plant a long kiss on your mouth! I can't wait to give you all, I can't wait! I can't! With love,".

What woman wouldn't like to receive letters like this? Is there any woman who wouldn't want her man to write to her expressing his love in a similar fashion? Perhaps the love of your life writes you love letters that make you feel special. Do you also write him messages to let him know that you appreciate him? For appreciation and respect are two things he needs to hear from you.

I kept wishing Alex might really be "the one," but I was skeptical, and for good reason. Was he a scammer? He never asked for money. It is possible he just wanted to be a pen pal. Who knows?

There were two red flags in Alex's letters: (1) he had to go abroad to meet with some clients of the investment company he worked for a week after we began communicating, and (2) he fell in love with me too quickly after we started chatting.

On August 16, Alex sent a very short note telling me that his beloved mother had died. Two days after that, I received the last letter from him. He was in anguish over her passing and described a little about what he was going through. The emails stopped abruptly, and I have not heard from him in since.

What was the motivation behind these letters, and why did he stop writing? Was he just playing a game? Who knows? His letters were different from all the others. They were definitely longer and more expressive, but he did not own a construction business, there was no emergency, and he did not ask for money, but the whole scenario was strange.

A few months later, I ran across some photos of a young US senator who had recently passed away. The man looked just like Alex, and there were several photos of the senator with other men who looked suspiciously like ones I had received from Alex.

I am sure that you are questioning my sanity, wondering why I subjected myself to all this drama, and at times, I have asked myself the same question. Yes, it was painful to find out they were just after my money. Even though I had suspected each one, the chats were very comforting, and for a short time, I lived the "romance." When each one ended, I grieved even though I felt betrayed. I grieved because I felt I had lost a friend, and that made me feel sad. I also felt angry with myself for wasting so much time and energy thinking about that person and writing responses to their emails.

I was mad at myself and embarrassed that I had sent Eugene money. I wanted to expose him and all the others. That is why I decided to write this book—to expose them. It became my passion to warn other people about the scammers and to remind them that they need to protect themselves physically, emotionally, and financially.

As I come to the end of my story, I realize how negative these last two chapters are, and I must explain that there are many decent and good men out there. I plan to continue my online search for my "Mr. Right." In spite of what you read here, I haven't given up.

I have chatted with over two hundred men whom the computers said matched me, and I have met about fifty of them. Several of them have become good friends. In addition, I have met several couples who found each other online and are now married. They are happy and say they are blessed, and I am happy for them.

During the same two years since I started my online search, I have dated only two men whom I met at the dances. I enjoy the dances and continue to attend them because it is good exercise. It is much easier, I think, to start a conversation with someone online than it is in person. The privacy of the internet helps to be a little bolder and easier for me to talk and flirt and have fun. Of course, one can take the time to think of a clever way to respond when texting, which is impossible to do in person. It is also easier to be the person we want to be, instead of the person we are, on the internet. We can appear to be more self-confident.

I have been disappointed only a few times with the men I have met. I was stood up only once, and I have had a lot of rejections. I have learned a lot from the experience, and I feel blessed. I am a survivor, and I know with each rejection I am brought a little closer to finding my one and only. I plan to relax more in the future and let God do the work for me. I definitely do not want to sound "needy" because I am not. I would like to have a companion, but I do not need one.

CHAPTER TWENTY-FOUR

What If?

The other night, I was able to sit down and watch a movie on television for the first time since I started writing this book. The name of the movie was *Letters to Juliet*, and it actually gave me the idea for an ending to my story. The story line involved a young female journalist who found a love letter lodged between two bricks in a wall of a city in Italy. Naturally, she read the letter and discovered the story of two young lovers from fifty years ago who had been separated by their parents and moved on to find new partners.

The main character decided to forward the letter to the woman and encouraged her to try to find her lost young love. The two women begin to search for the man, and in the end of the movie, the journalist wrote the following tribute for their wedding, which she reads. It is entitled "What if?"

Two words: *what* and *if.* When used separately, each word has its own meaning, but when used together, the phrase means something else entirely. *What* asks for information specifying something or for the repetition of something not understood, and *if* introduces a conditional clause, such as "on the condition or supposition that. . ." or "in the event that. . ." However, when used together, the phrase asks a question: What if I had chosen that path instead of this one? What if he changes his mind?[1]

Have you ever considered "what if" you had done something differently? Robert Frost's most famous poem, "The Road Not Taken," discusses this situation.

> Two roads diverged in a yellow wood, And sorry I could not travel both And be one traveler, long I stood And looked down one as far as I could

> To where it bent in the undergrowth; Then took the other, as just as fair, And having perhaps the better claim Because it was grassy and wanted wear;

> Though as for that the passing there Had worn them really about the same, And both that morning equally lay In leaves no step had trodden black.

> Oh, I kept the first for another day! Yet knowing how way leads on to way I doubted if I should ever come back. I shall be telling this with a sigh

> Somewhere ages and ages hence: Two roads diverged in a wood, and I, I took the one less traveled by, And that has made all the difference.[2]

Many years ago, when I first read this poem, I was struck by the profoundness of its truth, and it still touches me. I know how difficult it sometimes is to make a decision and then wonder if it was the right one. Somehow, when I look back on my life, I see that most of the time, my decisions were good ones. But I still wonder what my life would have been like if I had taken the other road.

Recently, I met a librarian who told me that after her first husband died, she had chosen to look up an old boyfriend. They began dating again, and now are happily married. She chose to find her first love and found out the answer to her "what if" question.

What about you? Perhaps it is time to answer your "what if" question. What if you meet the person of your dreams and live happily ever after? What if you do not? What if you are happy being single? What if you take that trip to Australia that you have been dreaming about? What if you don't? Now is the time to do whatever it is you want to do and to go wherever you want to go. If not now, when? Probably never.

The End (or is it?)

EPILOGUE

September 10, 2020

I am taking the liberty of adding this update. Three months ago, I was attempting to begin a marketing campaign to sell my first book so I opened an Instagram account. The pandemic caused a lockdown that has lasted almost the entire year and the things I had been doing, Meet the Author and Book Signing events, ceased. What I discovered was that, accidentally, I was on a free dating site inside Instagram, and suddenly a bunch of guys began wanting to chat with me.

In the four months since then, I have received over seventy-five requests to chat. I have met none of them, however, and I do not intend to meet them. They all fall in one of the following categories:

All of them have exhibited the red flags I listed in chapter 21.

Most claim to be in war zones on a peacekeeping mission and are in the war zones.

Four have claimed to be doctors.

Several have been business men working overseas and unable to come home due to the pandemic.

About five have been working here in the USA.

Ten have been engineers working on oil rigs in the Gulf of Mexico, near UK, and in the North Sea.

There have been about eight who claimed to be generals. One chatted for several weeks even after I told him I was currently in a relationship. "We can still be friends," he wrote. Eventually he got around to his "story." He had received orders to go into enemy territory with his men and they expected to have casualties. Should he not make it out alive, he wanted me to get in touch with his twelve-year-old son or daughter (I forgot which), and bring her or him to the USA to live with me until he turned twenty-one. At that time the child would receive the inheritance that would then be paid by the government and I would receive whatever it had cost me during those nine years. How ridiculous! I had told him my age, seventy-eight. What a stupid idea. I refused and he harassed me until I blocked him.

However, a month or so later another general contacted me who also had a twelve-year-old child. I requested a photo and received the exact same photo the first general had sent me. Can you believe it? I told this guy about this and then I blocked him.

Please be careful out there! Do not be taken in by these criminals and do not send them what they ask for. Also please be careful what you tell them because they are recording it and will use that in the future to find your weak spot.

I wish all of you the best. Protect yourselves physically, emotionally and financially. May God bless you.

NOTES

1. Vivian Greene, *Goodreads Inc*, (2017), Accessed August 21, 2018, https://www.goodreads.com/quotes/132836-life-isn-tabout-waiting-for-the-storm-to-pass-it-s-about.
2. Wikipedia.com, s.v., "online romance scams," accessed November 1, 2020, https://en.wikipedia.com/wiki/Online_romance_scams.

Chapter Three

1. Wikipedia.com, s.v., "grief," accessed August 1. 2020. http://www.wikipedia.com/browse/grief.
2. Earl A. Grollman, *"Earl A. Grollman Quotes,"* accessed December 15, 2019, https://www.azquotes.com/author/64158-Earl_A_Grollman.
3. Ibid.
4. Darby Faubion, *"The 7 Stages of Grief: What they are and How They Affect you,"* accessed June 23, 2020, https://www.regain.us/advice/general/the-7-stages-of-grief-what-they-are-and-how-they-affect-you/.
5. Janis Leslie Evans, "Cardinal Spirit," accessed January 15, 2020, https://letterpile.com/poetry/Spirit-Visits-From-Loved-Ones-Cardinal-Spirit-Poem.
6. The Holy Bible, KJV, Revelation 21:4.
7. The Holy Bible, KJV, Genesis 2:18.

Chapter Four

1. OxfordDictionairies.com, s.v., "regurgitate," accessed October 31, 2018, https://en.oxforddictionaries.com/definition/regurgitate.
2. Albert Einstein, *Brainy Quote*, accessed June 21, 2018, https://www.brainyquote.com/quotes/albert_einstein_121993.

Chapter Six

1. The Holy Bible, KJV, Genesis 1:1-31.
2. Michael Fiore, *"The Magnetic Online Dating Mindset,"* Online Allure, Module 1, Lesson 2, http://digitalromanceinc.com, 2013.

Chapter Seven

1. Marni Kinrys, "Turn Yourself On in Order to Turn Him On," *That's Not How Men Work,* (Venice, CA, 2017), www.thatsnothowmenwork.com, 65-79.

Chapter Nine

1. Vocabulary.com, s.v. "attract," accessed, September18, 2018, https:/www.vocabulary.com/dictionary/attract.
2. Kevin P. Ryan, the Business Insider, Axel Springer SE, 2009, https://www.businessinsider.com/.
3. Ibid.

Chapter Ten

1. Oxford Living Dictionaries, s.v. "love," accessed August 20, 2018, https://en.oxforddictionaries.com/definition/love.
2. Roman Krznaric, *"The Ancient Greeks' 6 Words for Love (And Why Knowing Them Can Change Your Life)",* Accessed December, 2018, https://www.yesmagazine.org/health-happiness/2013/12/28/the-ancient-greeks-6-words-for-love-and-why-knowing-them-can-change-your-life/.
3. Vocabulary.com, s.v. "with," accessed, September18, 2018, https:/www.vocabulary.com/dictionary/with.
4. Thesaurus.com, s.v. "in love with", accessed Marcy 9, 2020, https://www.thesaurus.com/browse/in%20love%20with.
5. Ibid. Krznaric.
6. Mirriam-webster.com, s.v. "infatuation," accessed August 20, 2018, https://www.merriam-webster.com/dictionary/infatuation.
7. Ibid, s.v. "lust," accessed August 20, 2018, https://www.merriam-webster.com/dictionary/lust.
8. Ibid, s.v. "affection," accessed August 20, 2018, https://www.merriam-webster.com/dictionary/affection.
9. Ibid, s.v. "passion," accessed August 20, 2018, https://www.merriam-webster.com/dictionary/passion.

10. The Holy Bible, NIV, I Corinthians 13:4-7.

11. Theresa E. DiDonato Ph.D., Psychologytoday.com, accessed October 31, 2018, https://www.psychologytoday.com/us/experts/theresa-e-didonato-phd, 2018.

12. Ibid.

13. Sabrina Alexis, "11 Undeniable Signs He's In Love With You," A New Mode, accessed October 31, 2018, https://www.anewmode.com/dating-relationships/signs-he-isin-love-with-you/5/, 2018.

14. Bella Pope, *Does She Love Me? 15 Signs She Actually Loves You,* accessed October 31, 2018, https://www.everydayknow. com/does-she-love-me/, 2017.

Chapter Eleven

1. Carlos Cavallo, Audio: *Understanding Men,* accessed May 1, 2018, https://www.datingadviceguru.com/catalog, 2017.

2. Ibid.

3. Ibid.

4. Bill and Pam Farrell, "Men Are Like Waffles - Women Are Like Spaghetti", 2001.

5. Ibid. Cavallo.

6. Ibid.

7. Ibid.

8. Ibid.

9. Ibid.

10. Ibid.

11. Ibid.

12. Ibid.

13. Ibid.

14. Ibid.

15. Ibid.

16. Ibid.

17. Ibid.

18. Ibid.

19. Steve Harvey, *Act Like a Lady, Think Like a Man,* First Ed. (New York: HarperCollins), 2009.

Chapter Twelve

1. Ibid, Cavallo.

Chapter Thirteen

1. WebMD.com, *"Understanding Sexually Transmitted Diseases (STDs),"* accessed August 19, 2018, http://www.webMD. com, 2017.
2. Ibid.

Chapter Fourteen

1. eHarmony.com, *"Dealing with Objections to your New Relationship from your Adult Children,"* accessed August 21, 2018, 2017, https://eharmony.com/dating-advice.
2. Ibid.
3. Ibid.
4. The Holy Bible, KJV, Genesis 2:24.

Chapter Fifteen

1. Dating Sites Reviews, accessed September 20, 2018, https://datingsitesreviews.com.
2. Michael Fiore, *"Online Dating Heaven, Online Dating Hell,"* Online Allure Module 1, Lesson 1," accessed April 24, 2018, https://digitalromanceinc.com.
3. Ibid. Fiore, *"The Five Kinds of Guys Who Use Online Dating,"* Online Allure Module 2, Lesson 1, accessed April 24, 2018, https://digitalromance.com.

Chapter Sixteen

1. Zoosk.com. *"Zoosk's First Study of Romance in 2018,"* accessed August, 24, 2018, https://www.datingsitesreviews.com/article.php?story=zoosk-s-first-study-of-the-year-revealsthe-state-of-romance-in-2018, Feb. 13, 2018.

Chapter Eighteen

1. https://www.consumer.ftc.gov/articles/0560-online-dating-scams-infographic, accessed June 19, 2020.
2. Wymoo Investigators, *"Romania Romance Scams Increase, Say Romania Private Investigators,"* accessed August 21, 2018. https://www.wymoo.com/contact-us, 2016.

Chapter Nineteen

1. Phil McGraw, "Dr. Phil Show," accessed September 10, 2018, https://www.drphil.com/shows/two-sisters-confronttheir-mom-who-says-shes-married-to-tyler-perry-can-karla-beconvinced-she-was-scammed, July 26, 2018.

Chapter Twenty

1. The Holy Bible, NIV, Jeremiah 17:9.
2. Johnny Mercer, "Fools Rush In," Wikimedia Foundation, January 29, 2020, en.wikipedia.org/wiki/Johnny Mercer, accessed November 9, 2020.

Chapter Twenty-Four

1. Movie, *Letters to Juliet*. Directed by Gary Winick. Performed by Amanda Seyfried, Gael Garcia Bernal, Vanessa Redgrave, accessed August 21, 2010, Prime Video, 2010.
2. Robert Frost, "The Road Not Taken," *Mountain Interval, (New York: Holt), 1916.*

BIBLIOGRAPHY

Alexis, Sabrina. *"11 Undeniable Signs He's in Love with You."* A New Mode. Accessed October 31, 2018. https://www.anewmode.com/dating-relationships/signs-he-is-in-love-with-you. 2018.

Cavallo, Carlos. Audio: *"Understanding Men."* Accessed May 1, 2018. https://www.datingadviceguru.com/catalog.

Dating Sites Reviews. Accessed September 20, 2018. https://datingsites reviews.com.

Dictionary.com.

DiDonato, Theresa E. Ph.D. Psychologytoday.com. Accessed October 31, 2018. https://www.psychologytoday.com/us/experts/theresa-e-didonato-phd. 2018.

Evangelical Lutheran Worship, Augsburg Fortress,(Minneapolis, MN), 2006.

eHarmony.com. *"Dealing with Objections to your New Relationship from your Adult Children."* Accessed August 1, 2018. http://eharmony.com./datingadvice.

Einstein, Albert. *Brainyquote.com*. Accessed June 1, 2018. https://www. brainyquote.com/quotes/albert_einstein_121993.

Evans, Janis Leslie. "Cardinal Spirit," accessed January 15, 2020, https:// letterpile.com/poetry/Spirit-Visits-From-Loved-Ones-Cardinal-Spirit-Poem.

Farrell, Bill and Pam, "Men Are Like Waffles - Women Are Like Spaghetti", 2001.

Faubion, Darby. *"The 7 Stages of Grief: What they are and How They Affect You."* accessed June 23, 2020. https://www.regain.us/advice/ general/the-7-stages-of-grief-what-they-are-and-how-they-affect-you/.

FBI. Accessed June 20, 2018. https://www.fbi.com.

Fiore, Michael. *"The Magnetic Online Dating Mindset,"* Online Allure, Module 1, Lesson 2, http://digitalromanceinc.com. 2013.

Fiore, Michael. *"Online Dating Heaven, Online Dating Hell."* Online Allure: Module 1. Lesson 2. Accessed July 21, 2018. http:// digitalromanceinc.com. 2013.

Fiore, Michael. *"The Five Kinds of Guys Who Use Online Dating,"* Online Allure Module 2, Lesson 1. Accessed April 24, 2018. https:// digitalromance.com.

Fiore, Michael. *"The Truth About Online Dating."* Online Allure: Module 1. Lesson 1. Accessed July 21, 2018. http://digitalromanceinc. com. 2013.

Frost, Robert. *Mountain Interval.* (New York: Holt). 1916.

Greene, Vivian. *Goodreads Inc.* Accessed August 21, 2018.https://www. goodreads.com/quotes/132836-life-isn-t-aboutwaiting-for-the-storm-to-pass-it's-about.

Grollman, Earl A. *"Earl A. Grollman Quotes,"* accessed December 15, 2019, https://www.azquotes.com/author/64158-Earl_A_Grollman.

Harvey, Steve. *Act Like a Lady, Think Like a Man.* (New York: Harper-Collins). 2009.

Kinrys, Marni. *That's Not How Men Work.* (Venice, CA, 2017). www.thatsnothowmenwork.com. P. 65-79.

Krznaric, *Roman. "The Ancient Greeks' 6 Words for Love (And Why Knowing Them Can Change Your Life)",* Accessed December, 2018, https://www.yesmagazine.org/health-happiness/2013/12/28/the-ancient-greeks-6-words-for-love-and-why-knowing-them-can-change-your-life/.

Letters to Juliet. Directed by Gary Winick. Performed by Amanda Seyfried, Gael Garcia Bernal, Vanessa Redgrave. Prime Video. 2010.

McGraw, Phil Dr. "Dr. Phil Show." July 26, 2018. Accessed September 10, 2018. https://www.drphil.com/shows/two-sisters-confront-their-mom-who-says-shes-married-to-tyler-perrycan-karla-be-convinced-she-was-scammed. 2018.

Mercer, Johnny. "Fools Rush In," Wikimedia Foundation. January 29, 2020. Accessed November 9, 2020. Accessed November 9, 2020.. en.wikipedia.org/wiki/Johnny Mercer.

Mirriam-webster.com.

OxfordDictionaries.com.

Pope, Bella. *"Does She Love Me? 15 Signs She Actually Loves You."* Accessed October 31, 2018. https://www.everydayknow.com/does-she-love-me/. 2017.

Ryan, Kevin. *The Business Insider.* Accessed August 21, 2018.(New York). 2009.

The Big Deer, *"The Significance Cardinal,"* accessed January 15, 2020, https://thebigdeer.com/what-does-it-mean-when-you-see-a-cardinal.

The Holy Bible. KJV. Genesis 1:1.
The Holy Bible. KJV. Genesis 1:27.
The Holy Bible. KJV. Genesis 1:31.
The Holy Bible. KJV. Genesis 2:24.
The Holy Bible. NIV. I Corinthians 13:4-7.
The Holy Bible, NIV, Jeremiah 17:9.
The Holy Bible. NJV. Revelation 21:4.
The Holy Bible. KJV. Revelation 24.4.

The United Methodist Hymnal, The United Methodist Publishing House, (Nashvillle, TN), 1989.

Thesaurus.com, s.v. "in love with", accessed Marcy 9, 2020, https://www.thesaurus.com/browse/in%20love%20with.

Vocabulary.com

Wikipedia.org.

WebMD.com. *"Understanding Sexually Transmitted Diseases (STDs)."* Accessed August 19, 2018. http://www.webMD.com. 2017.

Wymoo Investigators. *"Romania Romance Scams Increase, Say Romania Private Investigators."* Accessed July 19, 2018. https://www.wymoo.com/contact-us. 2016.

Zoosk. *"Zoosk's First Study of Romance in 2018.* Datingsitereviews.com. Accessed April 24, 2018.https://datingsitesreviews.com. 2018.

ABOUT THE AUTHOR

Shelby Wagner is a professional who cares. A retired music teacher, Wagner was born in Arkansas, and she grew up in Michigan where she married and raised two children. She has a BA and a BMus from Oakland University and a MA from Michigan State University. Her biography was posted in Marquis' Who's Who in the Midwest, 1990-1991 Edition.